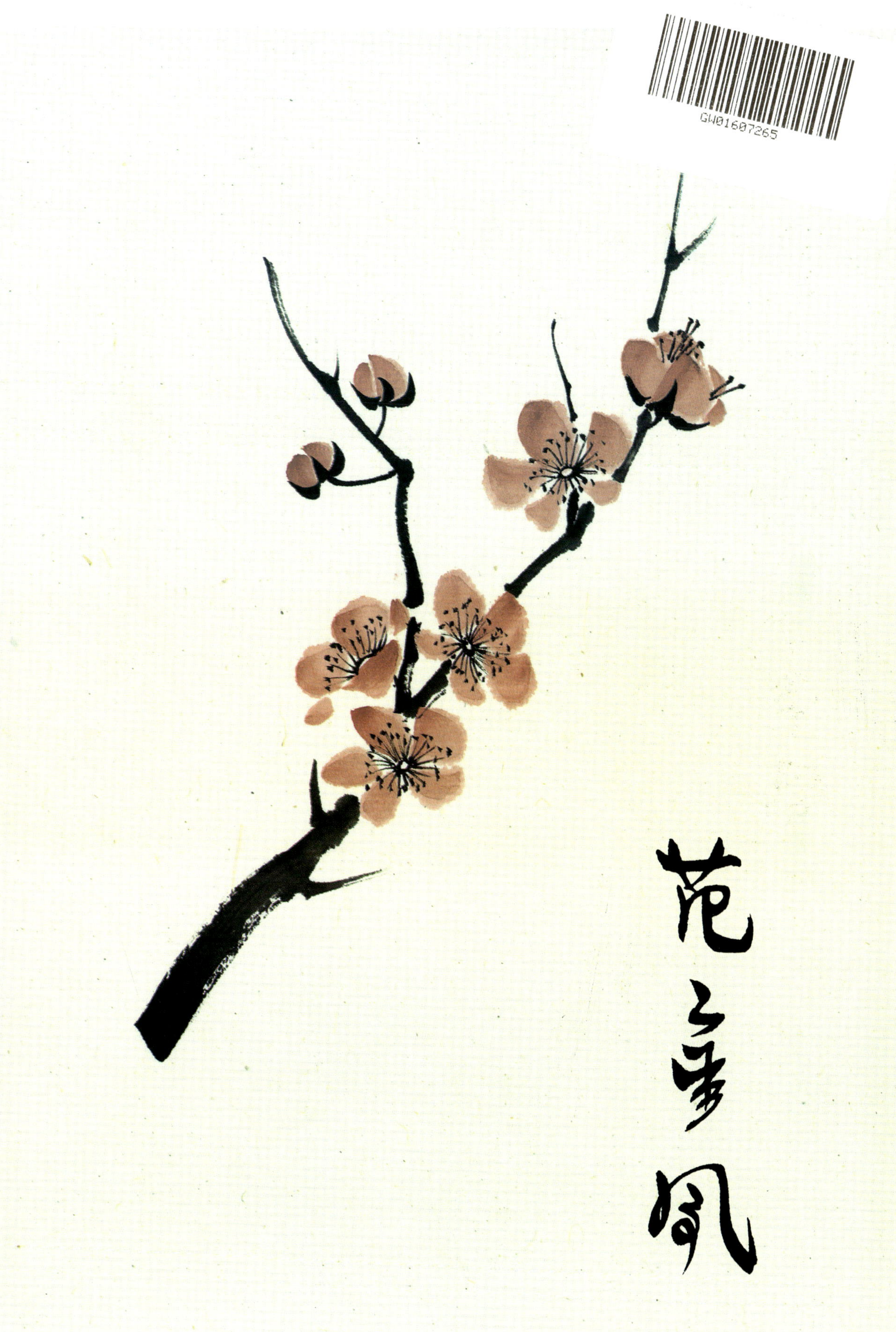

Contents

Introduction

I hope that by now you are hooked on Chinese painting! In this book I shall introduce you to colour. However, one must remember that brush control is of primary importance. Colour should be used sparingly. After all many Chinese artists paint only in shades of black. The other purpose of this book is to give you more ideas on how to develop your own painting style. I have therefore kept the compositions simple and have included a few Western subjects. I feel strongly that the Chinese, with their affinity to nature, would want us to draw some of our inspiration from what we see around us.

Although Chinese painting is based on copying, do remember it is the technique you are copying rather than the actual subject. If you copy too precisely from another picture your painting will be too stiff and lack the essential 'chi' (vitality) of Chinese painting. Study a picture, then look away and produce your own interpretation.

Also important at this stage is sketching. Although one never draws on the final painting, one should go out and sketch the subjects around you at every opportunity — whether they are flowers, landscapes or creatures — because in sketching you observe closely and commit your subjects to memory.

On the first few compositions in the book I have included a step by step guide. However, I have omitted this as the book progresses as I feel you will have familiarised yourself with the strokes and therefore will be able to work out for yourself which strokes are needed. When you first sit down to paint always practise brush strokes for about ten minutes to achieve a calm state of mind. When you start to make up your own compositions don't expect a perfect result the first time. Many an experienced artist will paint a subject many times before he is entirely satisfied. Now relax and enjoy your painting.

Maggie Cross
OCTOBER 1990

The Four Treasures

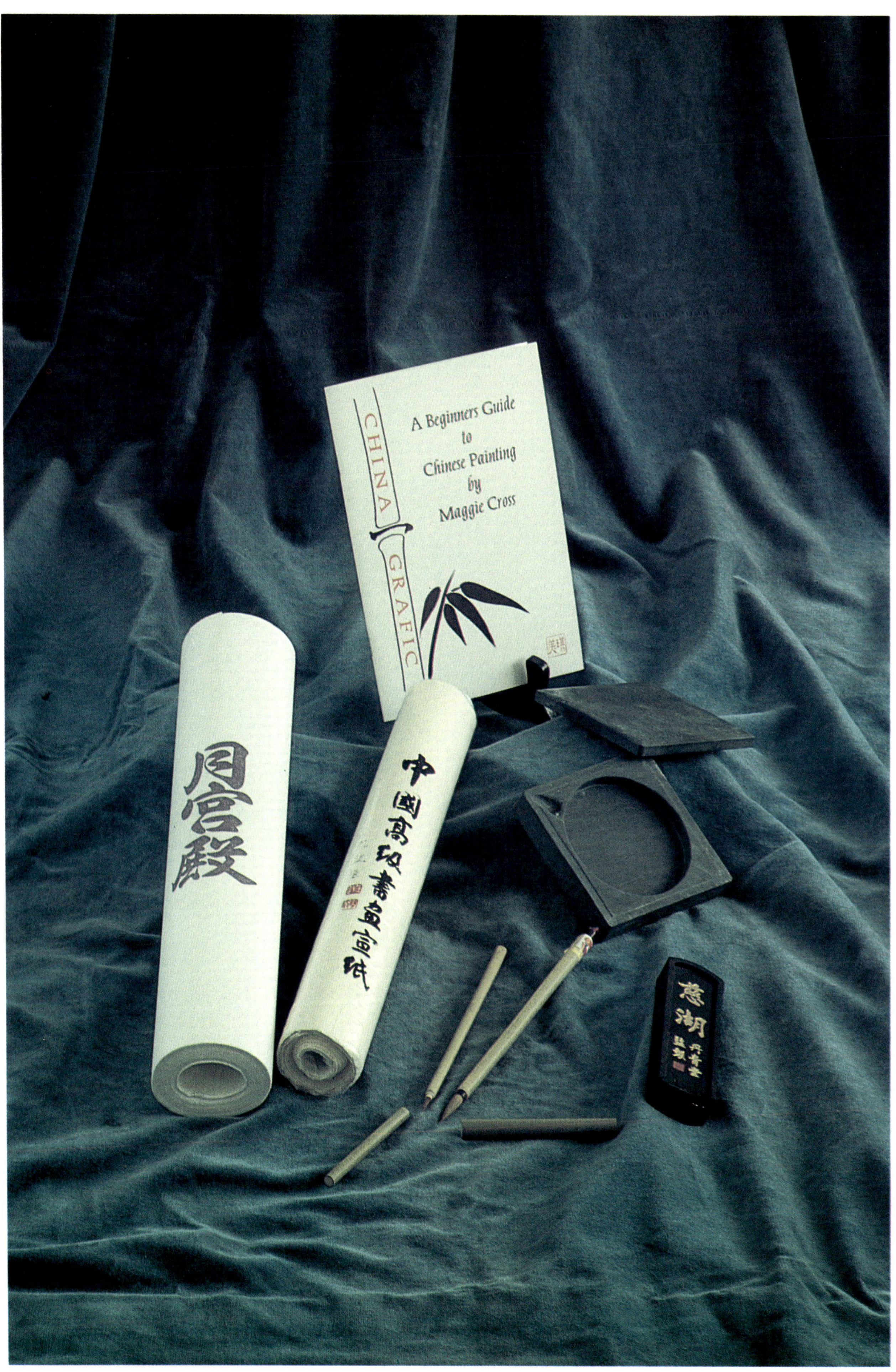

The Four Treasures

In Chinese painting your four treasures consist of a brush, an inkstick, an inkstone and paper. The full details regarding their care and use can be found in Book 1. However, I should like to remind you of a few important points. When you have removed the cap from your brush and soaked it in cold water, do not replace it as this will damage the bristles. The brushes come in many thicknesses and are made from various types of animal hair including goat, sheep, wolf, leopard, horse, rabbit and badger. At this stage you may wish to purchase some extra brushes.

The white haired are sheep or goat. These are absorbent and are suitable for calligaphy, short strokes like blossom and washes.

The fine brown haired brushes may be wolf or rabbit. They are much more flexible and easy to use, especially for long tapering strokes. Horse and badger hair brushes are coarser and not suitable for the paintings in this book.

The inksticks, which are made from soot and glue, come in many different qualities. The general rule is that the more you pay the better the quality. Never leave your inkstick standing on your stone when you finish grinding your ink as it will stick fast.

Inkstones are generally made of slate. I prefer the square ones with a cover which should be replaced when the stone is not in use. This prevents the ink from drying out and also keeps out the dust. It is important to wash your inkstone when you finish your painting for the day as grit may build up around the edges. Do not use abrasives. While grinding your ink close your eyes and relax for a few moments to achieve peace and tranquility!

The paper, which is generally obtainable by the roll, but may also be purchased in sheets, is called rice paper but can also be made from cotton, mulberry or bamboo fibres. It is sold in different degrees of absorbency for different types of painting. 'Moon Palace' is Japanese paper. It is white and shiny on one side, rough on the other. It is best to paint on the shiny side. The 'HSUAN' paper is a creamy colour and is sold in several long sheets on a roll. I prefer to paint on this paper. You will often notice slight flaws and wood chips in the paper. This is because it is handmade. I feel it makes it more interesting. I have used this paper for the paintings in this book.

Of course you also need newspaper or a cloth to lean on when painting, a paint rag to dab excess paint from your brush and 2 water pots — one for washing, one for rinsing.

Additional Equipment

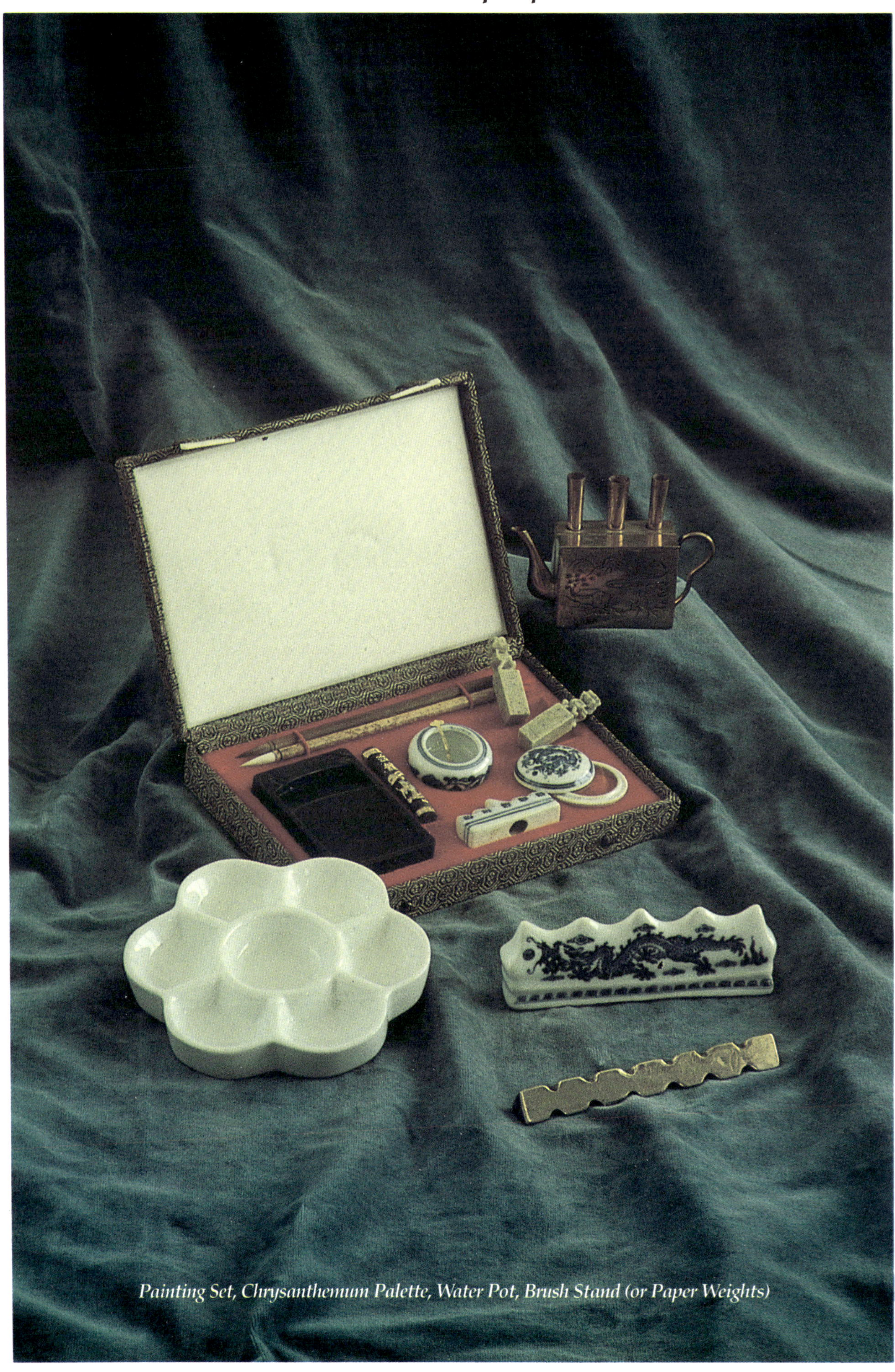

Painting Set, Chrysanthemum Palette, Water Pot, Brush Stand (or Paper Weights)

Additional Equipment

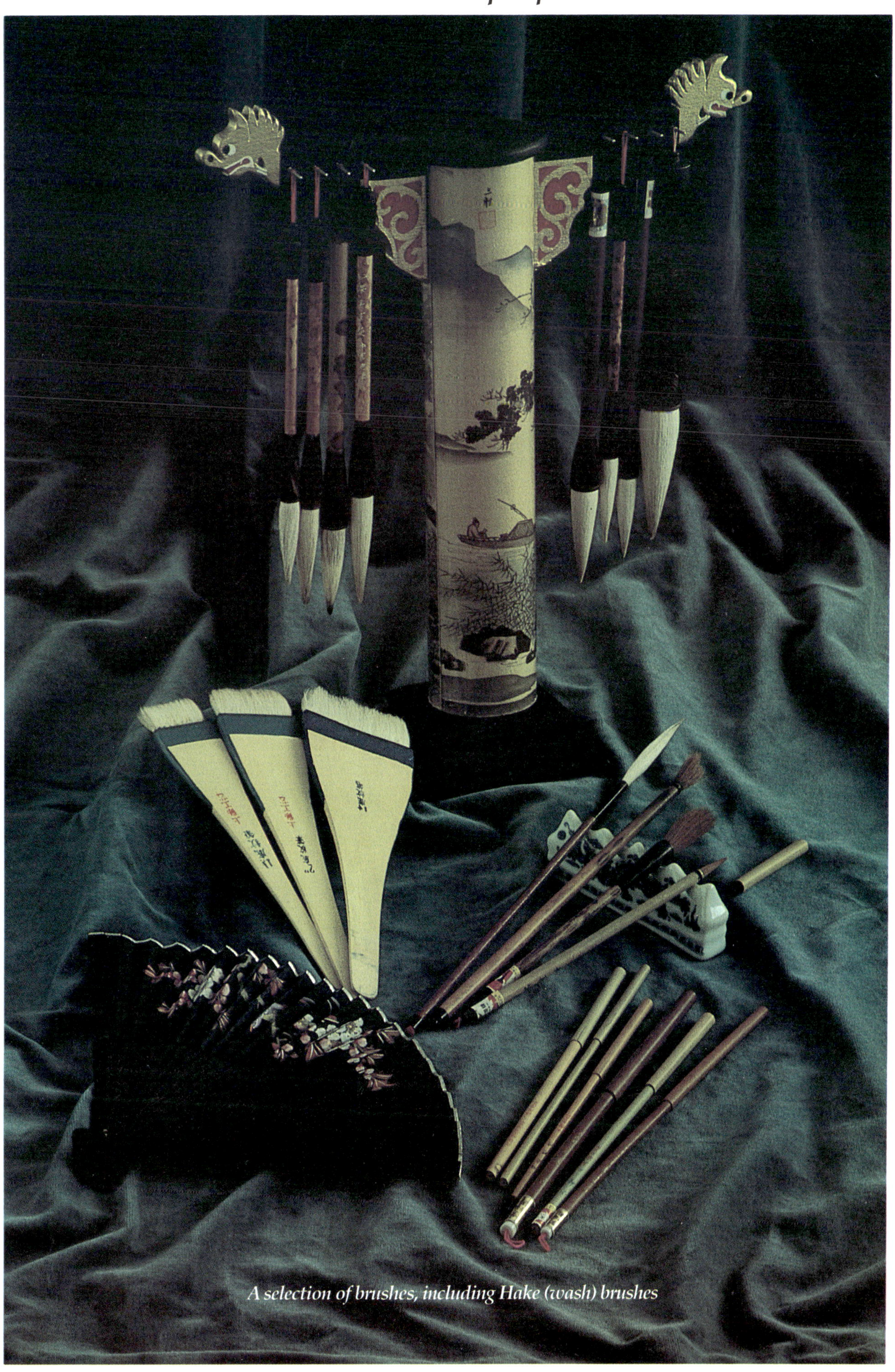

A selection of brushes, including Hake (wash) brushes

Chops and Seals

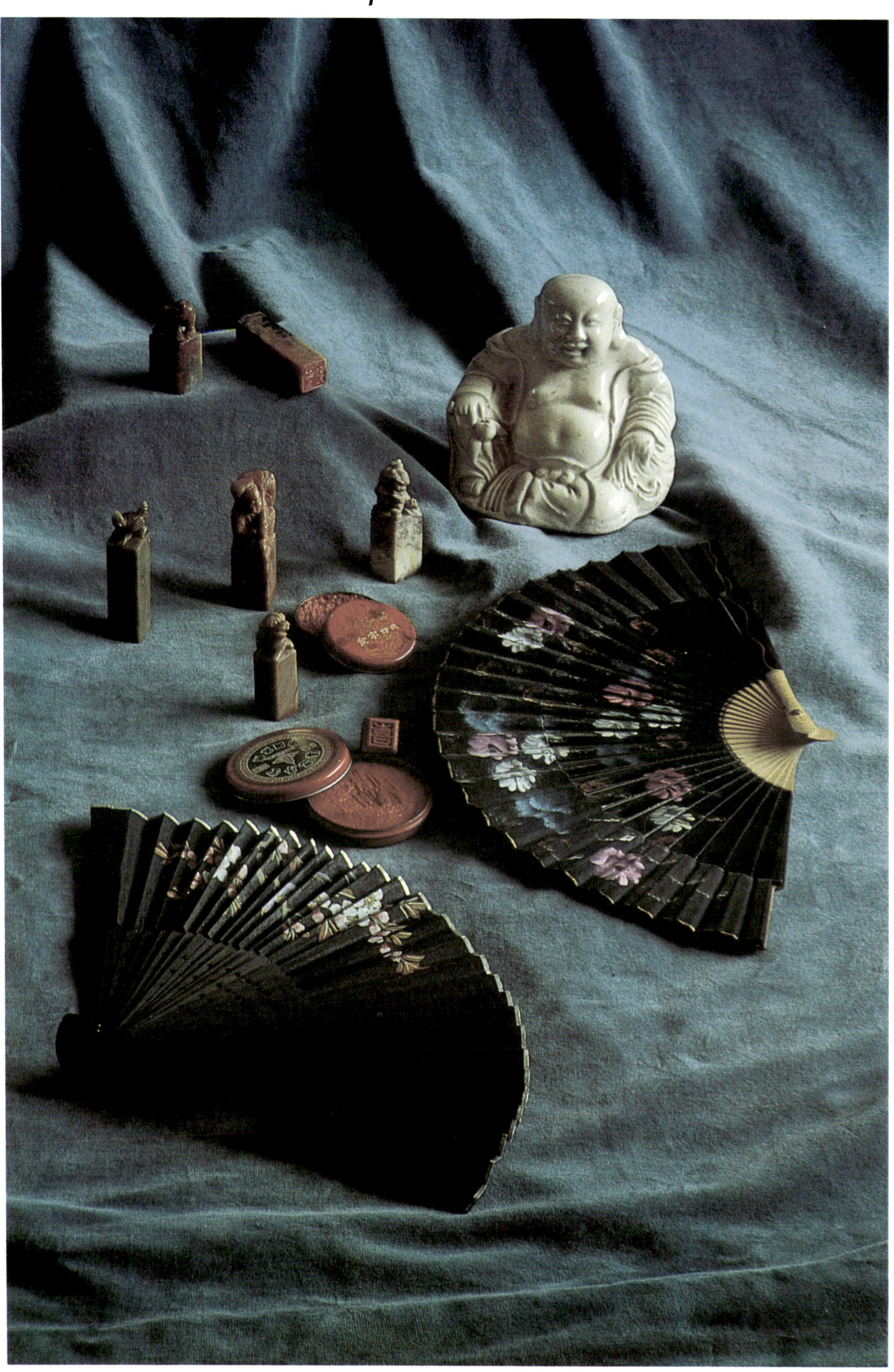

Chops and Seals

All Chinese paintings have a seal on them produced by the 'chop'. It may be in red lettering with a white background or white lettering with a red background.

The seal is generally the name of the artist. However as the Chinese have been avid collectors of paintings for centuries the seal may be that of a previous owner or even another artist to show his approval. Seals may also be the characters for the season, the year of the artist's birth or various lucky characters. Seals are generally carved from jade or soapstone with a decorated top and have become collectors items.

The chop is pressed into a red sticky paste called Cinnabai to produce the seal on the painting.

"I paint what I like"
Chi Pai Shi

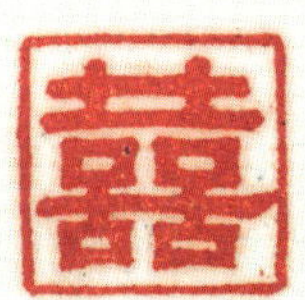

Double Happiness

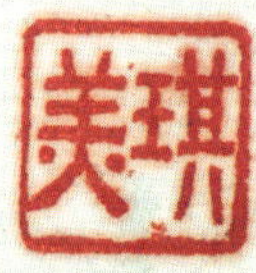

Author's
Western name

"Best Wishes"

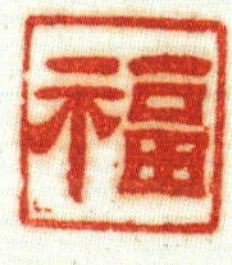

Good Luck

Author's
Chinese name

Colours

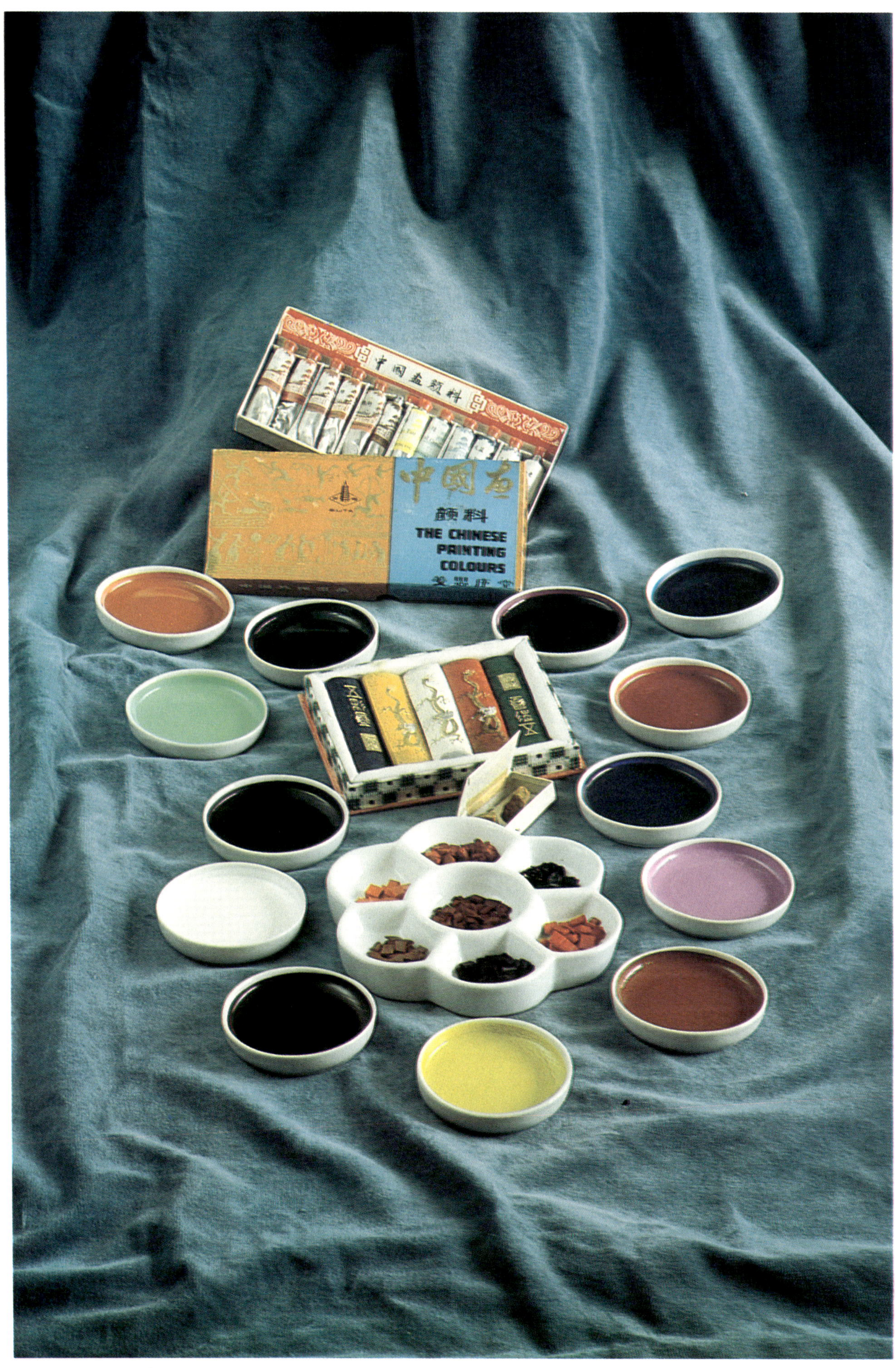

Colours

Colours for Chinese painting come in four different forms as illustrated on Page 10. The main difference between them and Western paints is that glue is added to the Chinese paints preventing them from running when a wash is added or they are wet mounted. For the illustrations in this book I have used Teppachi and crystal colours.

Tubes are used, as in the West. The colours are good, but their disadvantage is that they are inclined to go hard in the tube.

Crystals or colour chips are excellent value but are not very easily obtained in this country. To use place two or three chips on a palette and add a small amount of water to stick them down. A strong colour will appear in a matter of seconds. After use leave them in the palette and dampen again for re-use. Warm water may be used if you have difficulty in obtaining a strong colour.

Coloured sticks are used in the same way as your black inkstick by placing a few drops of water on a clean inkstone (a piece of roofing slate will do!) and grinding until the colour appears. (Time is the inconvenience here — dare I say it!)

Teppachi colours are Japanese. They are imported by Inscribe and can be purchased at most art shops. The colour is in a china palette and needs only to be dampened with your brush to obtain a good colour.

Do not lick your brush as some colours are poisonous.

Getting Started

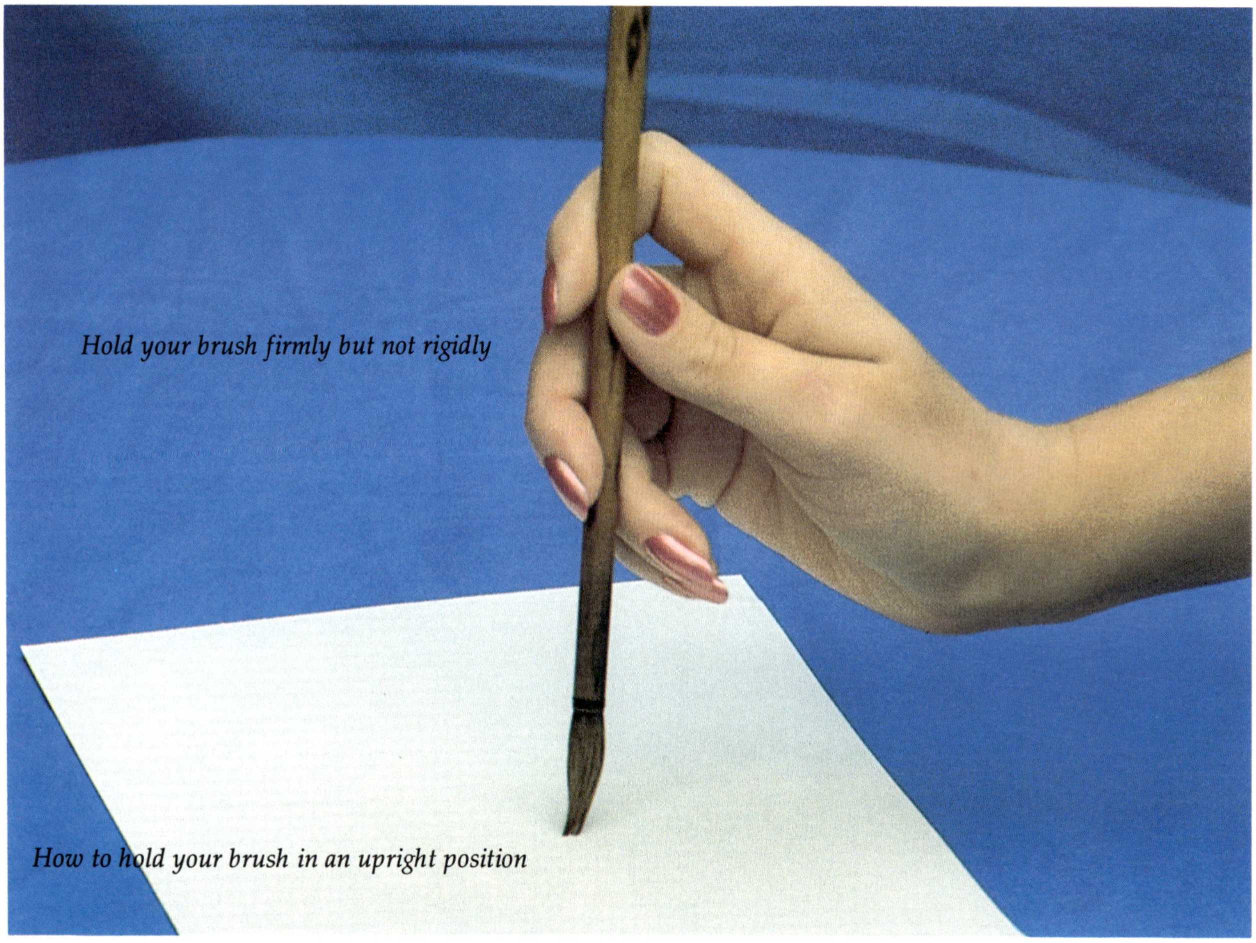

Hold your brush firmly but not rigidly

How to hold your brush in an upright position

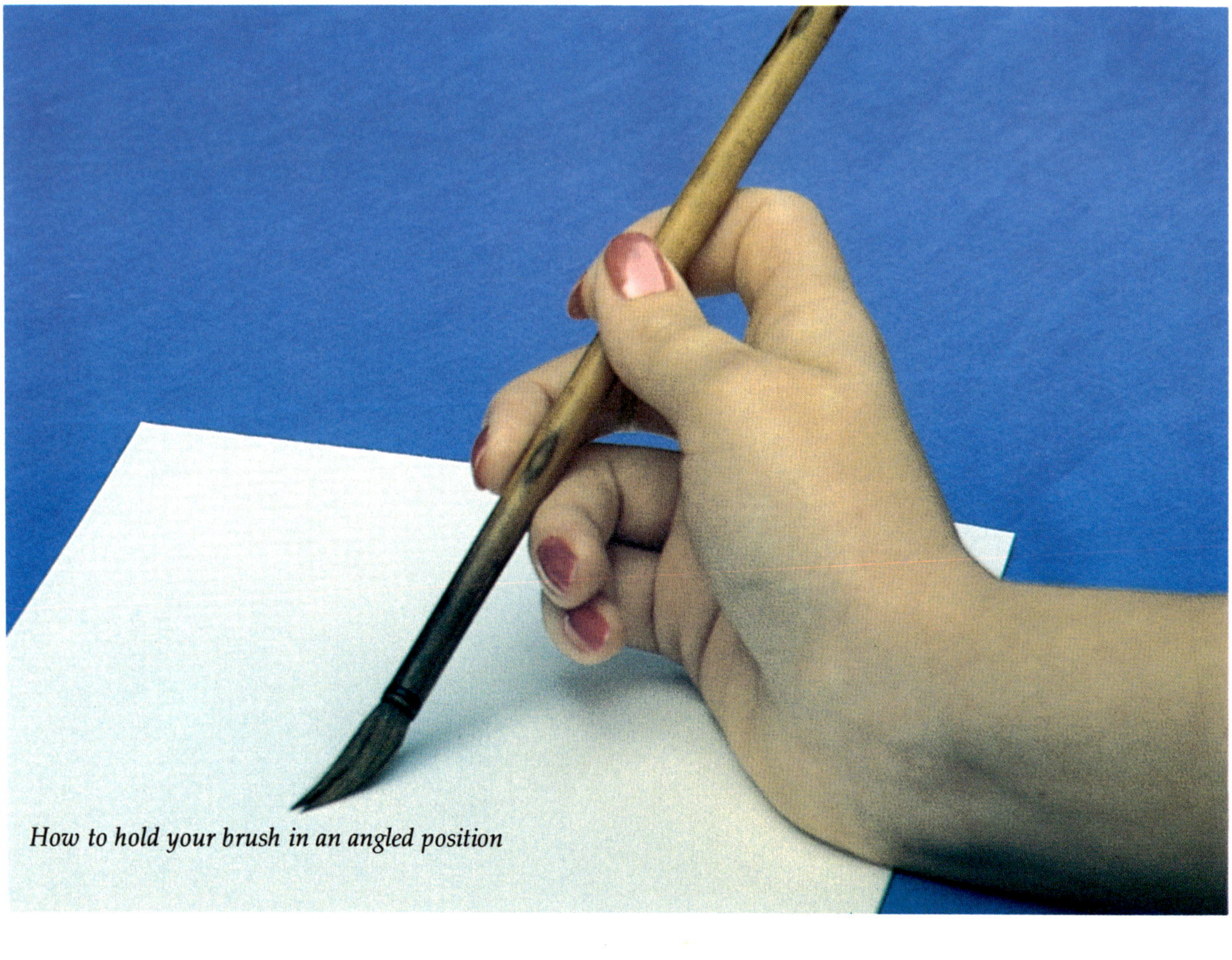

How to hold your brush in an angled position

Getting Started

On this page I have included the strokes you will need to master to paint the pictures in this book. (Notice how a stroke can be adapted to become a leaf, a boat or a bird's wing.)

Press lightly for fine strokes and harder for thicker strokes. Try to practise the gradual increase in pressure. For the wider strokes you may also use the brush at an angle as shown on the previous page. On some strokes I have rolled the brush in pale ink and pressed the tip into dark ink to achieve a shaded effect.

1. Upright Brush

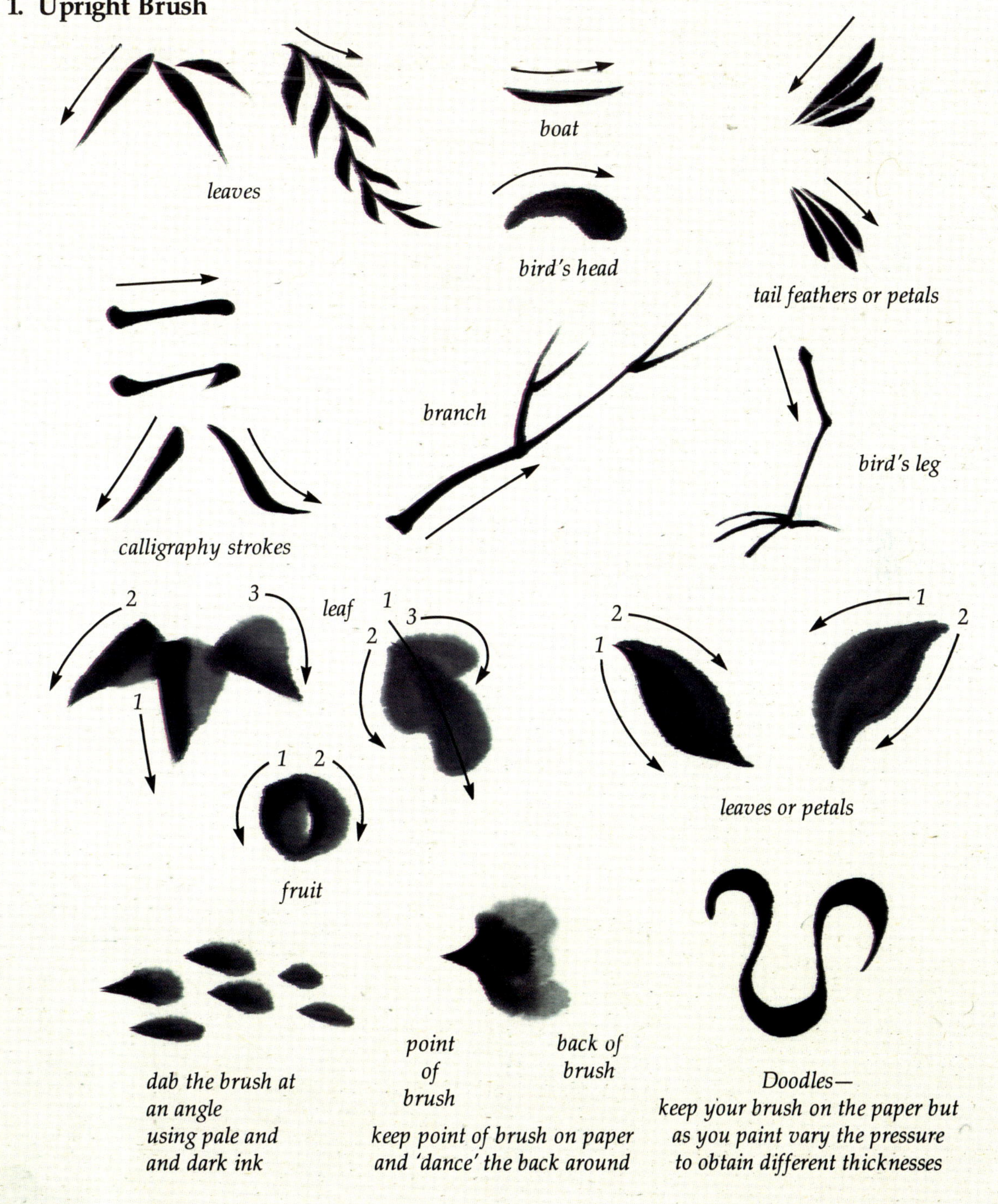

Black Ink Study

Composition of orchid and bamboo using different shades of black. Dilute the ink with water in your palette to obtain lighter shades.

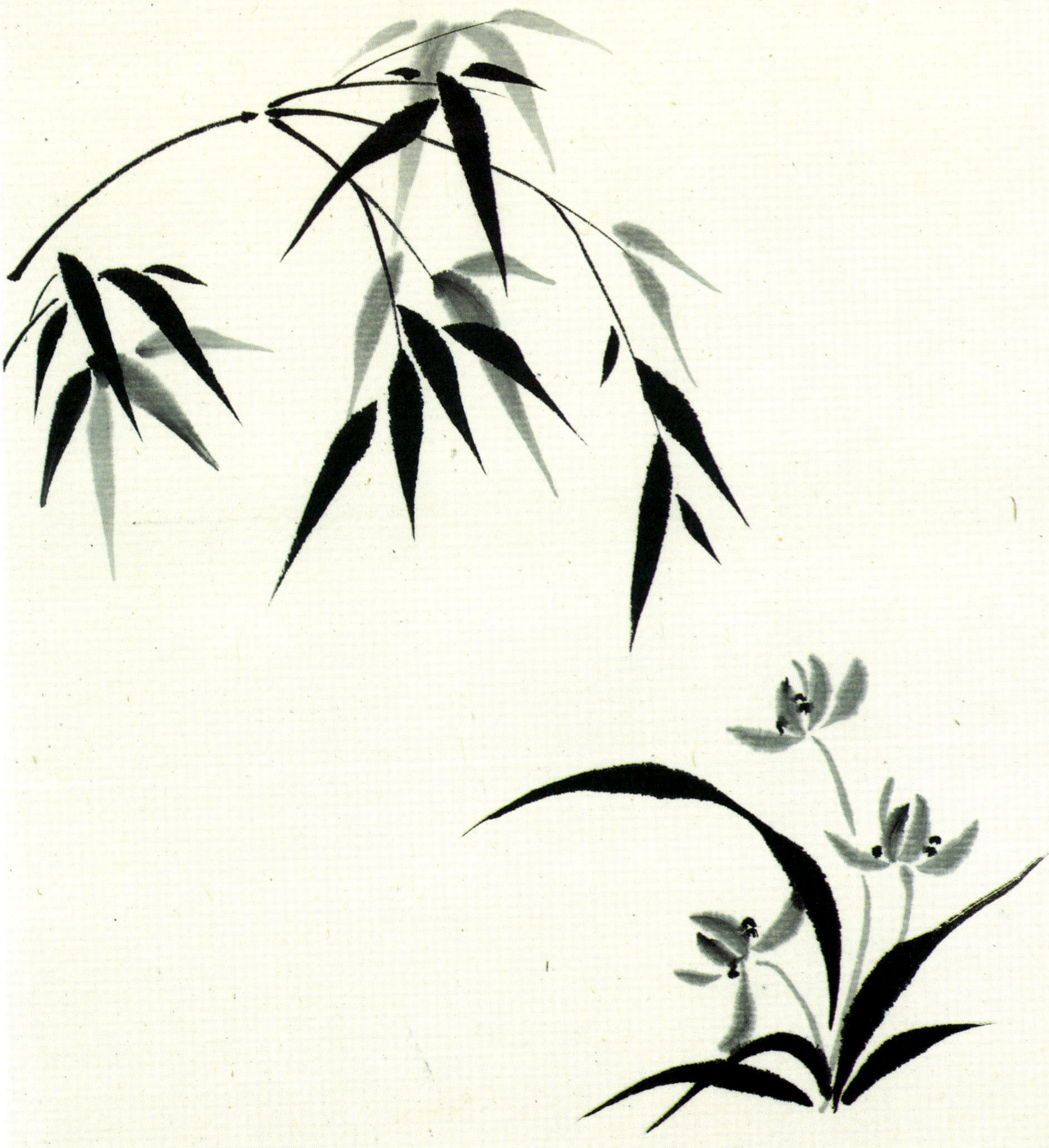

Starting with Colours

Spend some time experimenting with colour mixing and shading yourself. By 'shading' I mean rolling your brush in a pale colour and then dipping the tip only in either a darker shade of the same colour or another colour (as illustrated below).

The flower petals are painted in Rattan Yellow crystals tipped in orange crystals with Sienna centres.

For both types of leaf I mixed Rattan Yellow with Indigo crystals and darkened the tip of the brush with Indigo.

The butterfly wings are Sky Blue crystals (pale tipped in dark). I added the markings in Sky Blue while the wings were still damp.

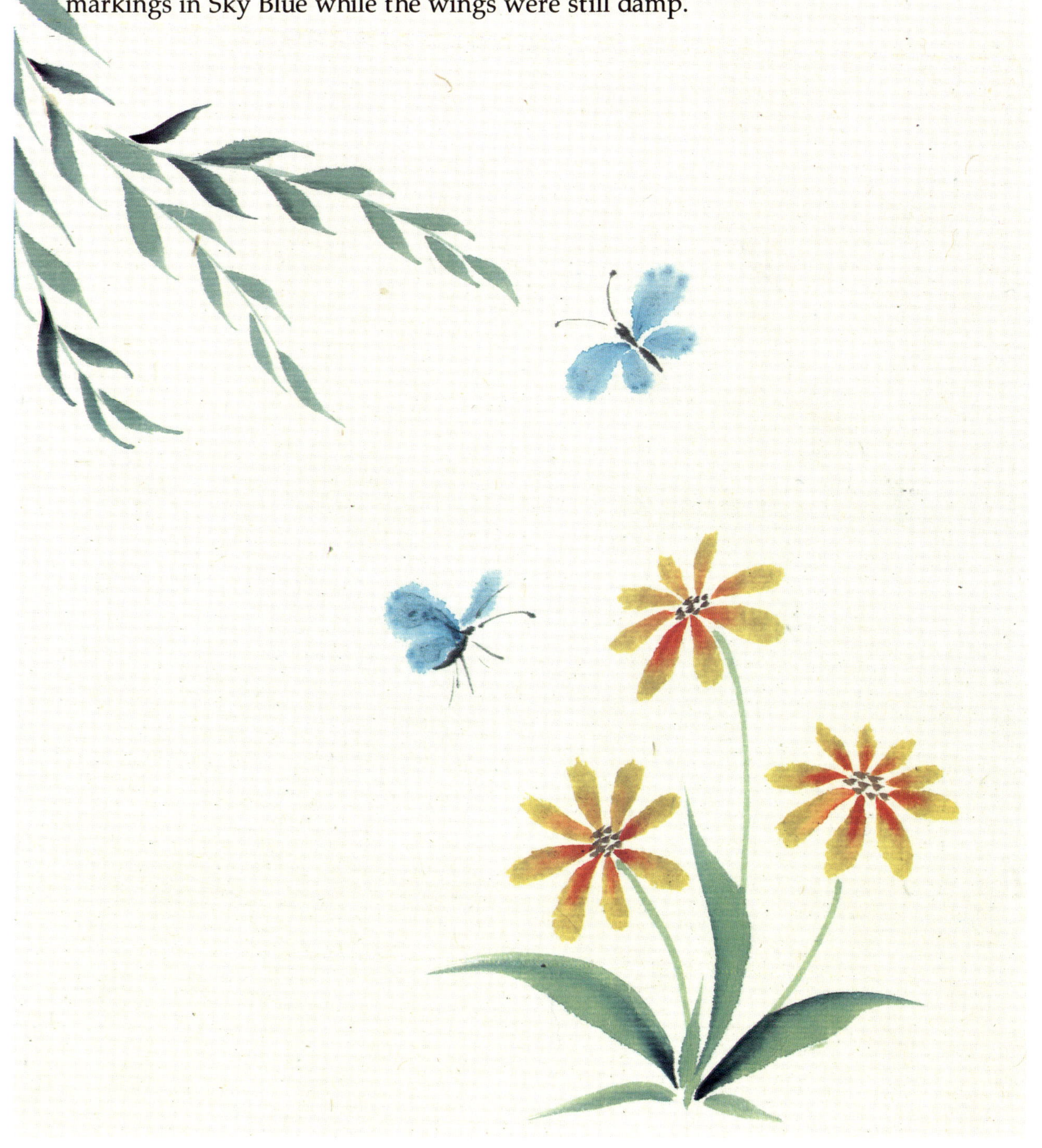

Squirrel with Grapes

I painted first the leaves, then the fruit and lastly the stems. Finally I added the squirrel. You will probably need to make several attempts at the squirrel. It is a good idea to sketch from life or photographs.

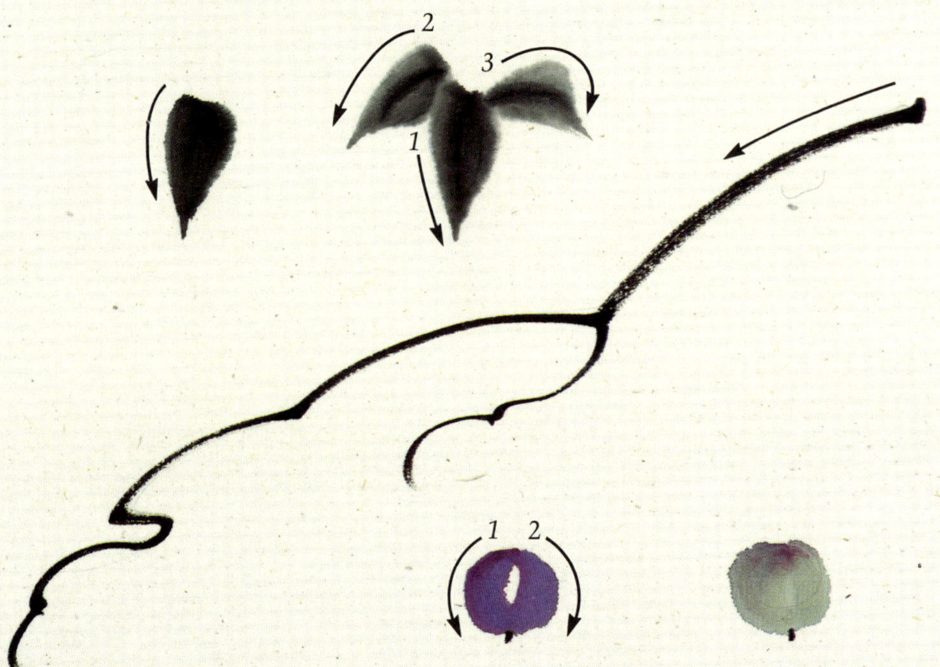

Leaves
Painted in shades of black ink. Start with your brush at an angle and as you paint the stroke lift the back of the brush so that it ends in an upright position. Paint on veins in dark ink while the leaves are slightly damp. When overlapping leaves take care as the colours may run.

Stems
Painted in black ink — holding brush upright, with very little ink on brush.

Fruit
Mix Sky Blue crystals with Peony Purple Teppachi to a light shade then push the tip of your brush into the neat Peony Purple. For the less ripe grapes I mixed a greeny colour with Rattan Yellow, Indigo and Sienna crystals and rolled my brush in this before tipping it in Peony Purple. Lean your brush slightly to one side.

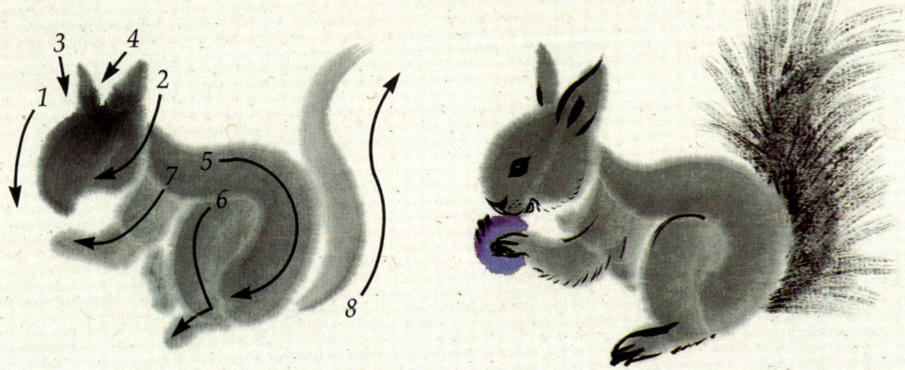

Squirrel
I painted the main shape (head, body, tail and legs) in pale grey ink, adding the details of eyes, fur, whiskers and claws in a darker ink when the grey was dry. To paint the fur split the brush hairs to create a ragged effect.

Squirrel with Grapes

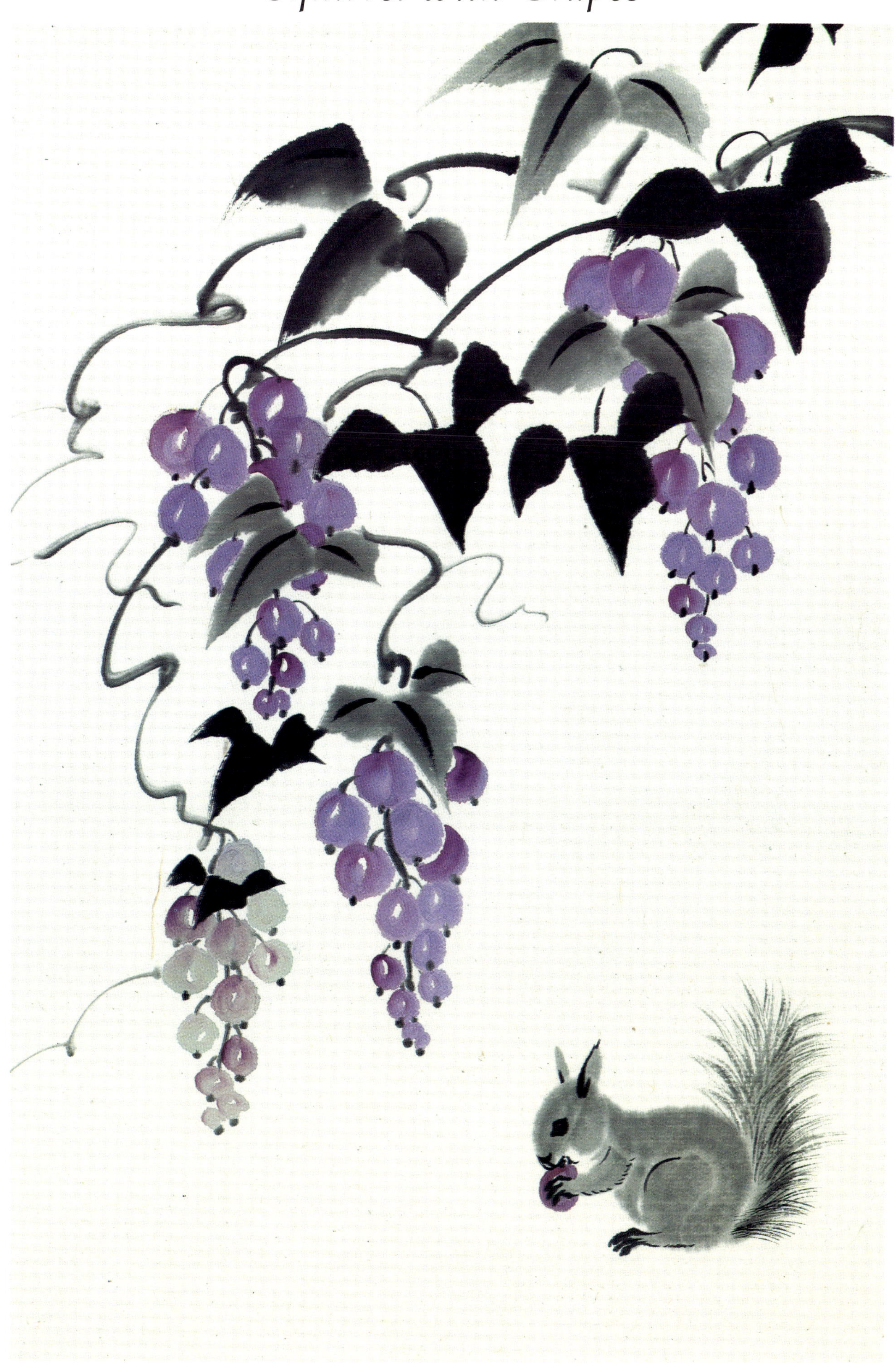

Blossom with Birds

It is easier to paint the bird first, then the branch and lastly the flowers. Apart from the flowers which are painted in Rough Red Chips the picture is painted in shades of black ink.

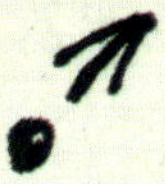

Paint the beak and eye first

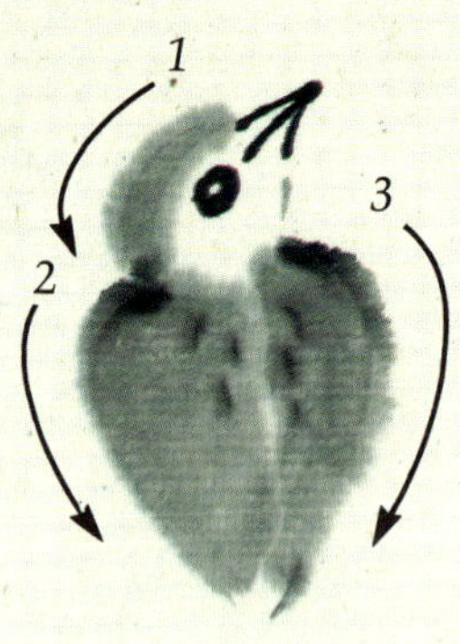

For head and wings lean brush to side

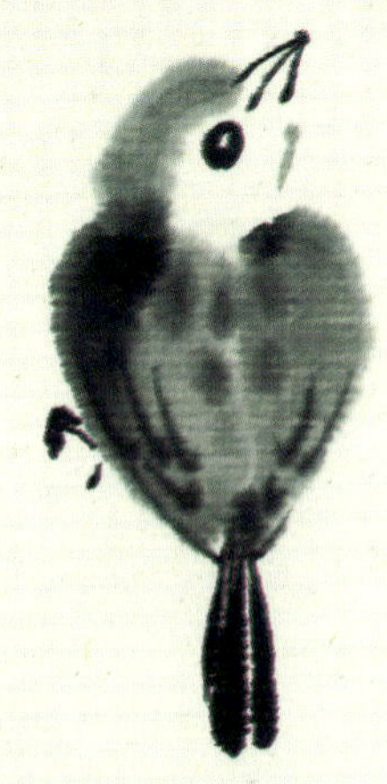

Add details of feathers and tail when previous strokes have dried

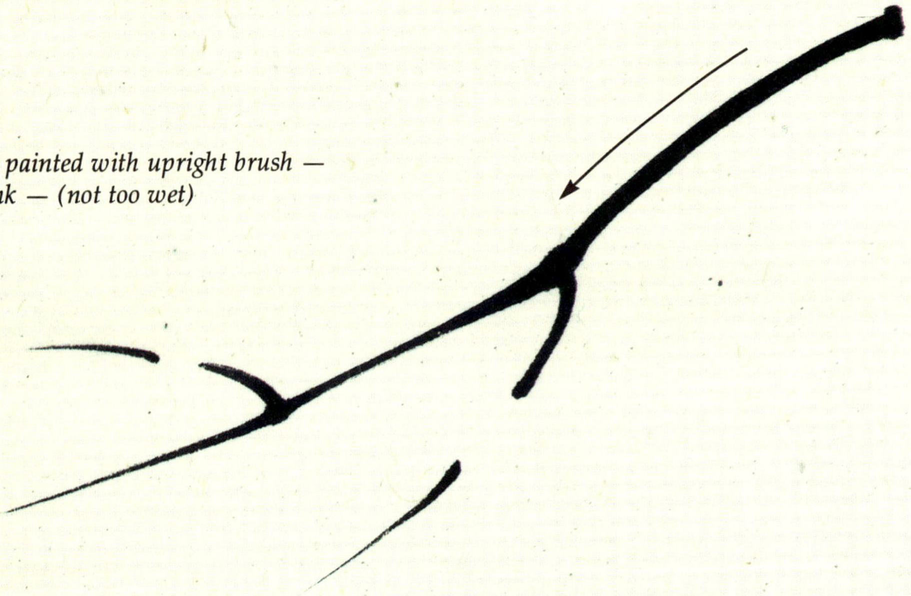

Branch painted with upright brush — black ink — (not too wet)

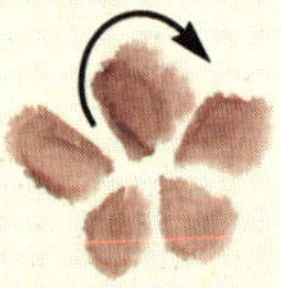

Blossom — upright brush follow directions of arrow, press lightly at outer edges of petal

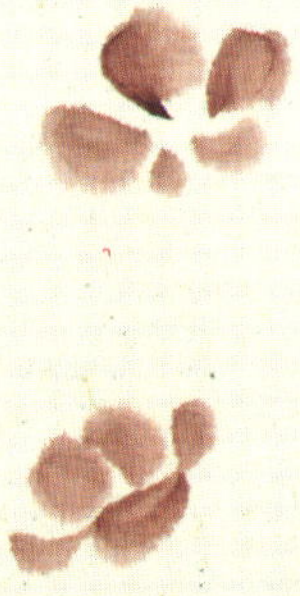

Fill brush with pale red and tip in neat paint

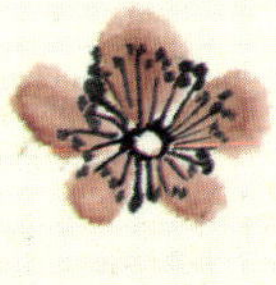

Add stamens when flower has dried

Blossom with Birds

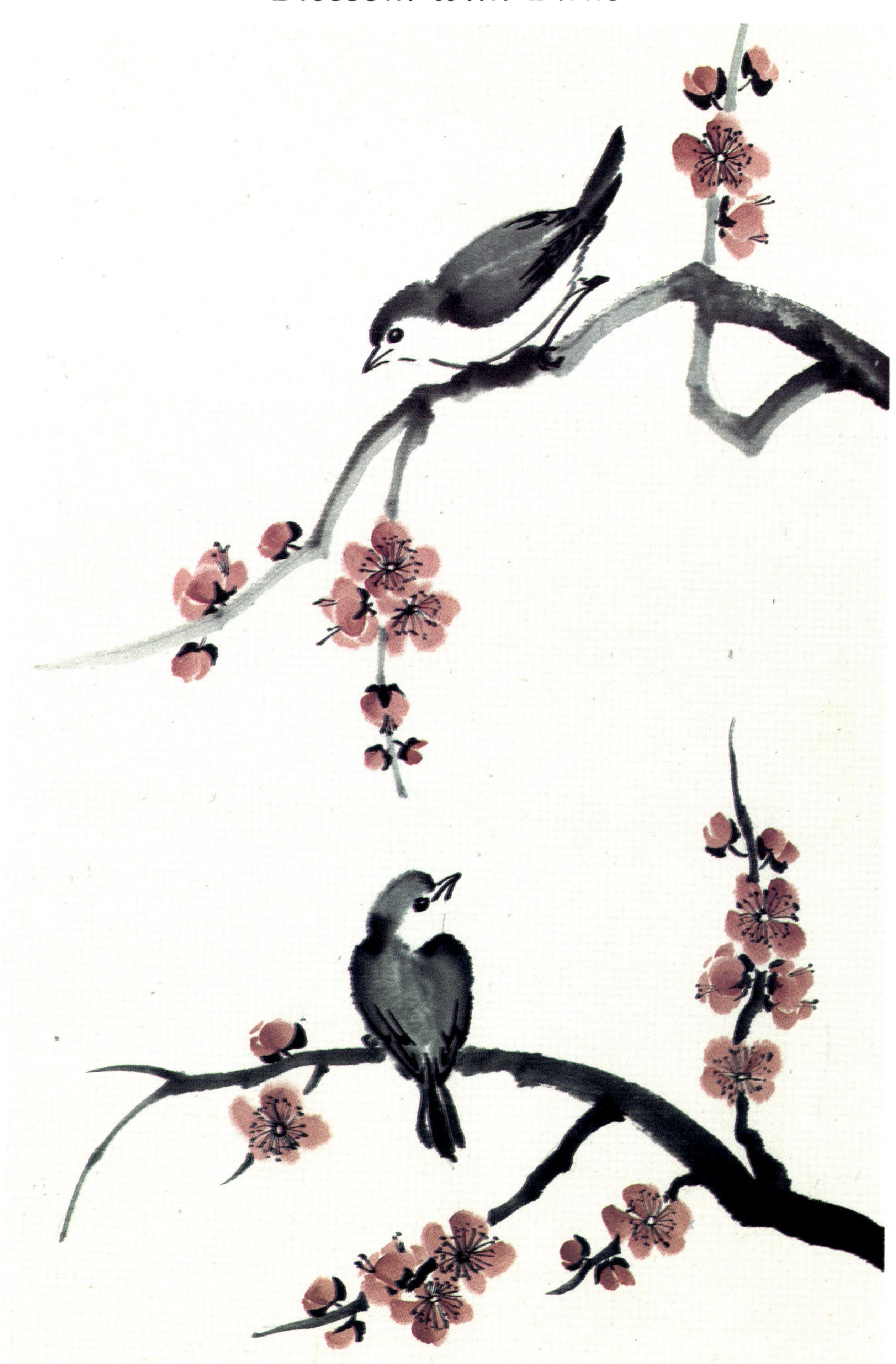

Chrysanthemum with Rabbit

For this painting I have used the 'Ku Fa' or outline style for the flowers.

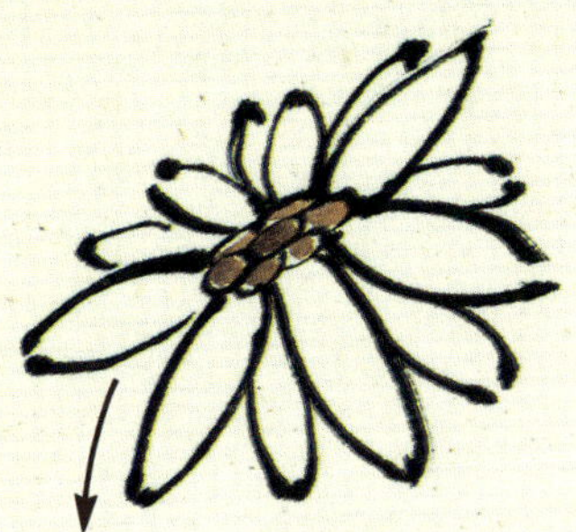

Outline the flowers and centres first then fill in the colour. For this I have used Rattan Yellow tipped in Sienna crystals and Sienna for the centre.

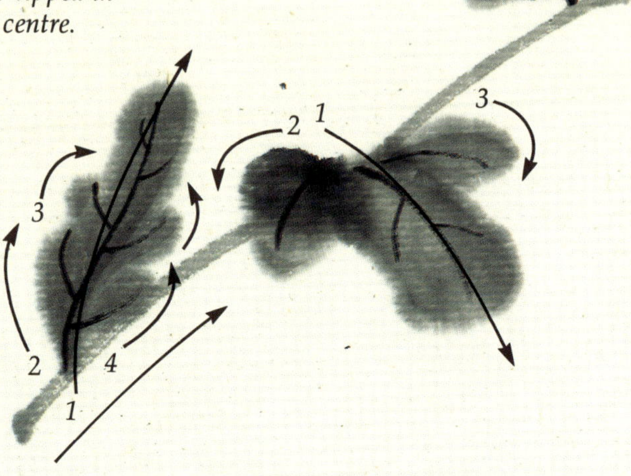

Paint the stems in pale ink, allow to dry slightly before adding the leaves. Paint the leaves in grey ink tipped in black. Hold your brush at an angle pressing lightly at first and increasing the pressure as you finish the stroke. Curve your brush round as it leaves the paper. Add dark veins when the leaves are still damp.

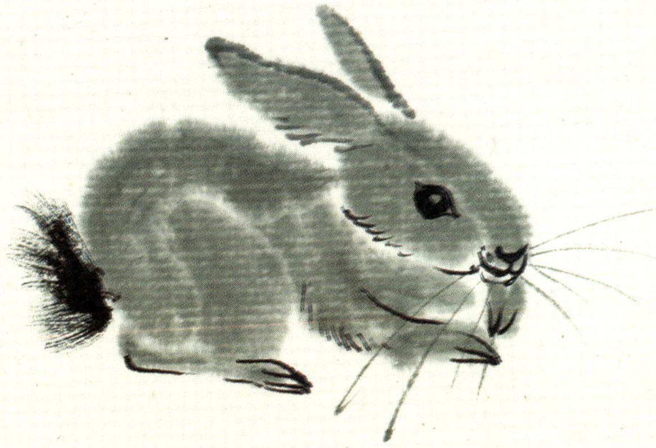

Rabbit
Follow the same instructions for painting the squirrel (page 16) for the rabbit.

I have chosen to paint a rabbit because the next year of the rabbit is 1999. I also spent some time sketching rabbits. — My thanks to Hannah!

Chrysanthemum with Rabbit

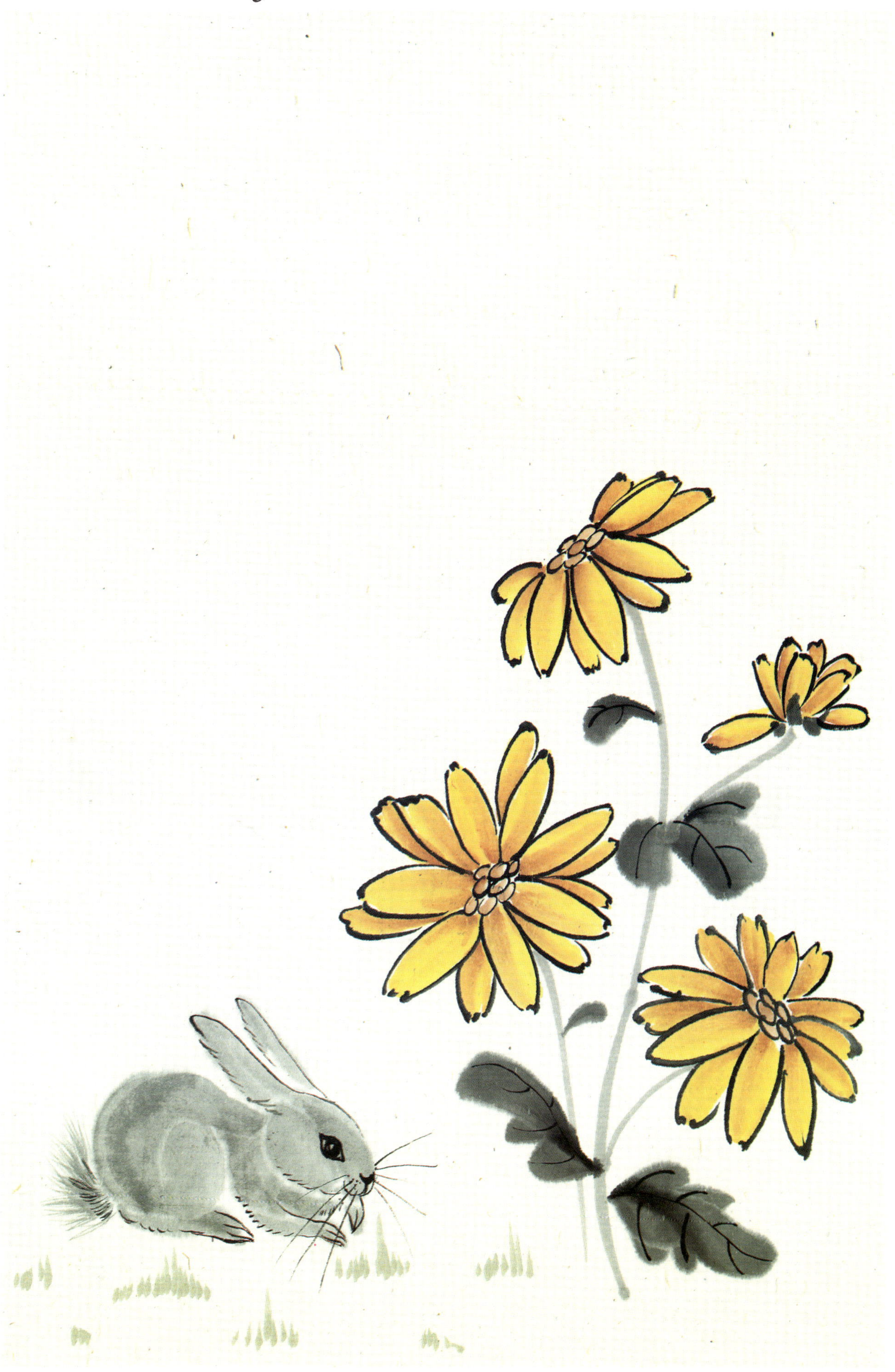

Chrysanthemum with Autumn Leaves

I have included two chrysanthemum paintings to show the 'Mo Ku' or non-outline style method as well as the 'Ku Fa' or outline style.

Paint the flowers first starting with the centre of the flower. Paint the petals from the outside towards the centre. I used Blood Red mixed with a very small amount of black and tipped in Rough Red crystals. Paint the centres with green then white.

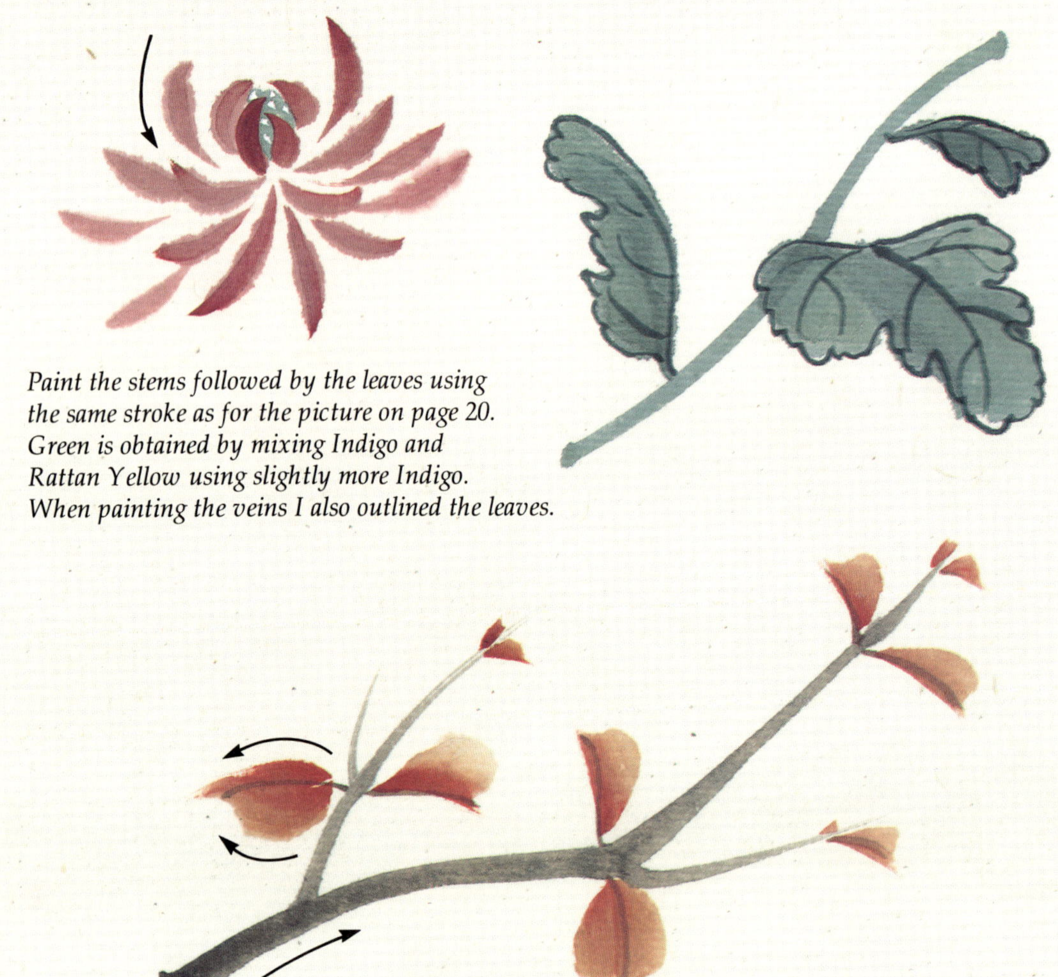

Paint the stems followed by the leaves using the same stroke as for the picture on page 20. Green is obtained by mixing Indigo and Rattan Yellow using slightly more Indigo. When painting the veins I also outlined the leaves.

Next paint in the autumn branches. The stems are in Autumn Brown and the leaves are Sienna crystals tipped in Dark Red crystals. Lean your brush slightly to the side when painting the leaves, decreasing the pressure to give you the shape.

I have also included a butterfly. Paint the body first in ink and paint the wings using a series of fine strokes. The colour is a mixture of Sienna and Bright Red chips.

Chrysanthemum with Autumn Leaves

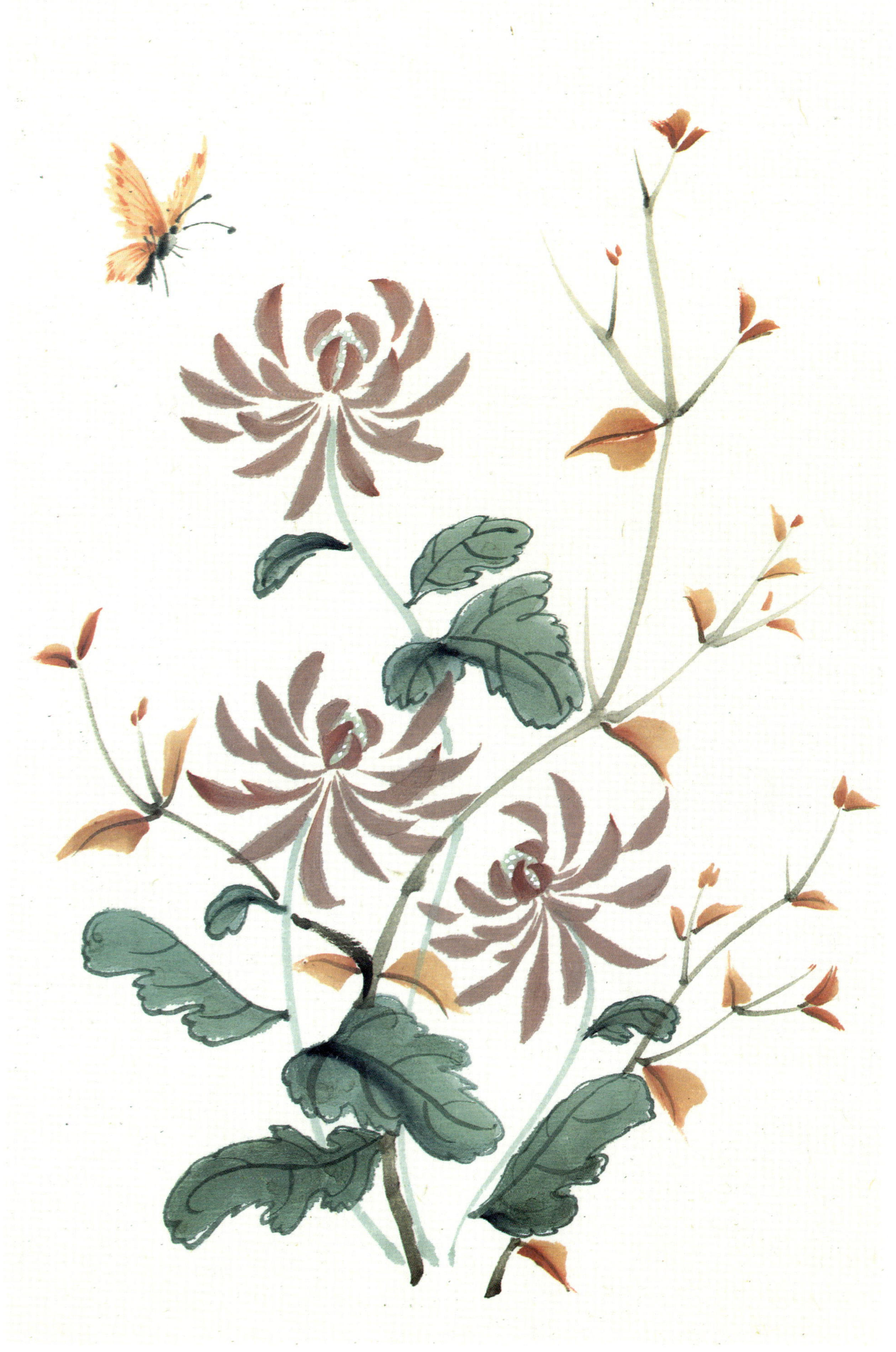

Wisteria with Duck

You will notice when looking at traditional Chinese paintings that certain subjects tend to be painted together. For example wisteria is often painted with fish, swallows or ducks.

Paint the flowers as illustrated using Peony Purple mixed with Sky Blue to create a pale shade and tip in pure Peony Purple. The lower lobes of the flower are painted in a mixture of Peony Purple and Blood Red with a dab of the brush. Add a dash of Rattan Yellow as indicated while still wet. Hold brush at a slight angle.

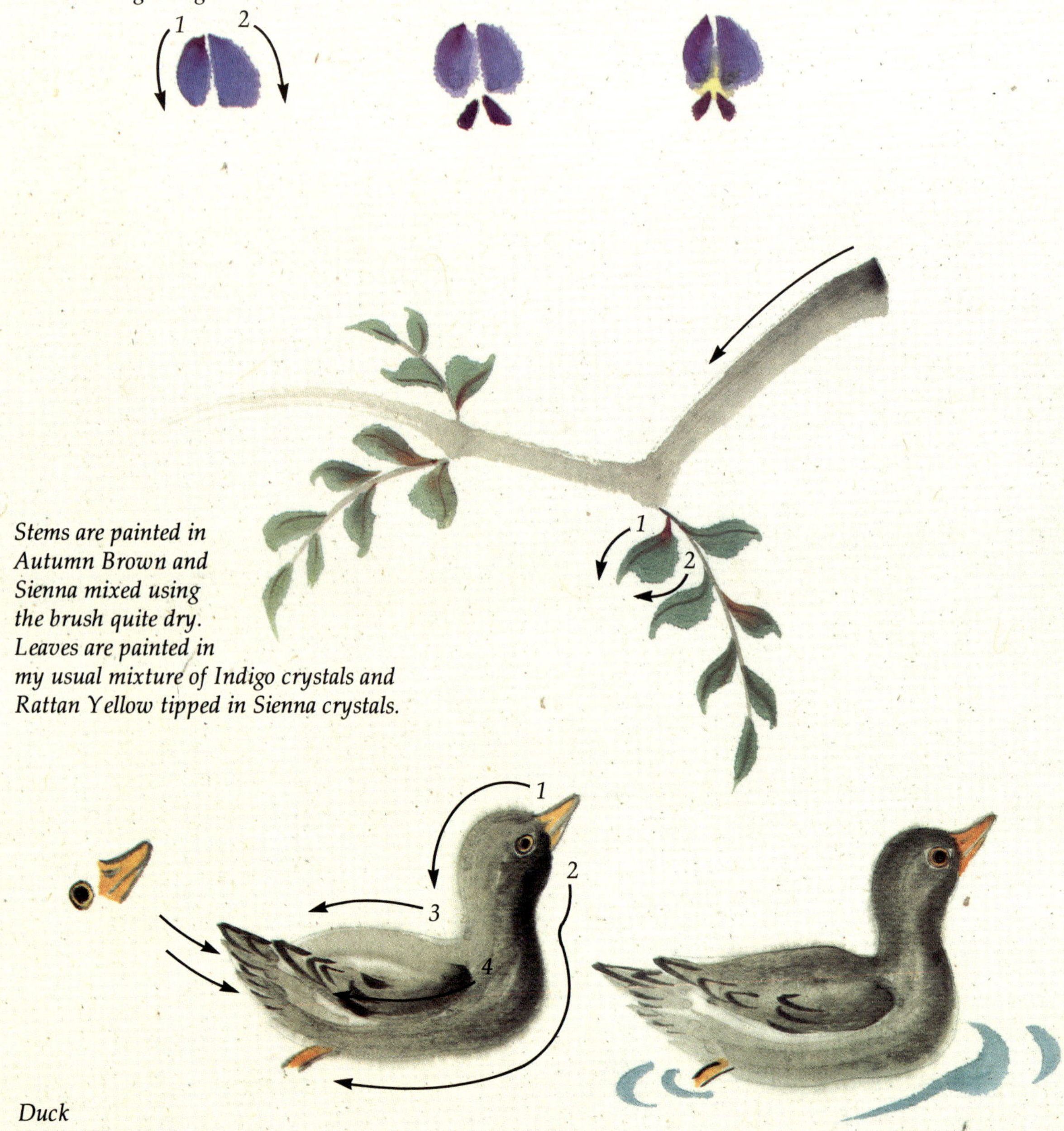

Stems are painted in Autumn Brown and Sienna mixed using the brush quite dry. Leaves are painted in my usual mixture of Indigo crystals and Rattan Yellow tipped in Sienna crystals.

Duck
Painted in pale Autumn Brown Teppachi with feather details added in a darker shade of the same colour. For the beak I used Rattan yellow mixed with a little Teppachi Vermillion. First paint the beak and eye then the body as indicated by the arrows. Finally add details when the paint is still slightly damp. For the final touch add some ripples of water in a very pale shade of Indigo.

Wisteria with Duck

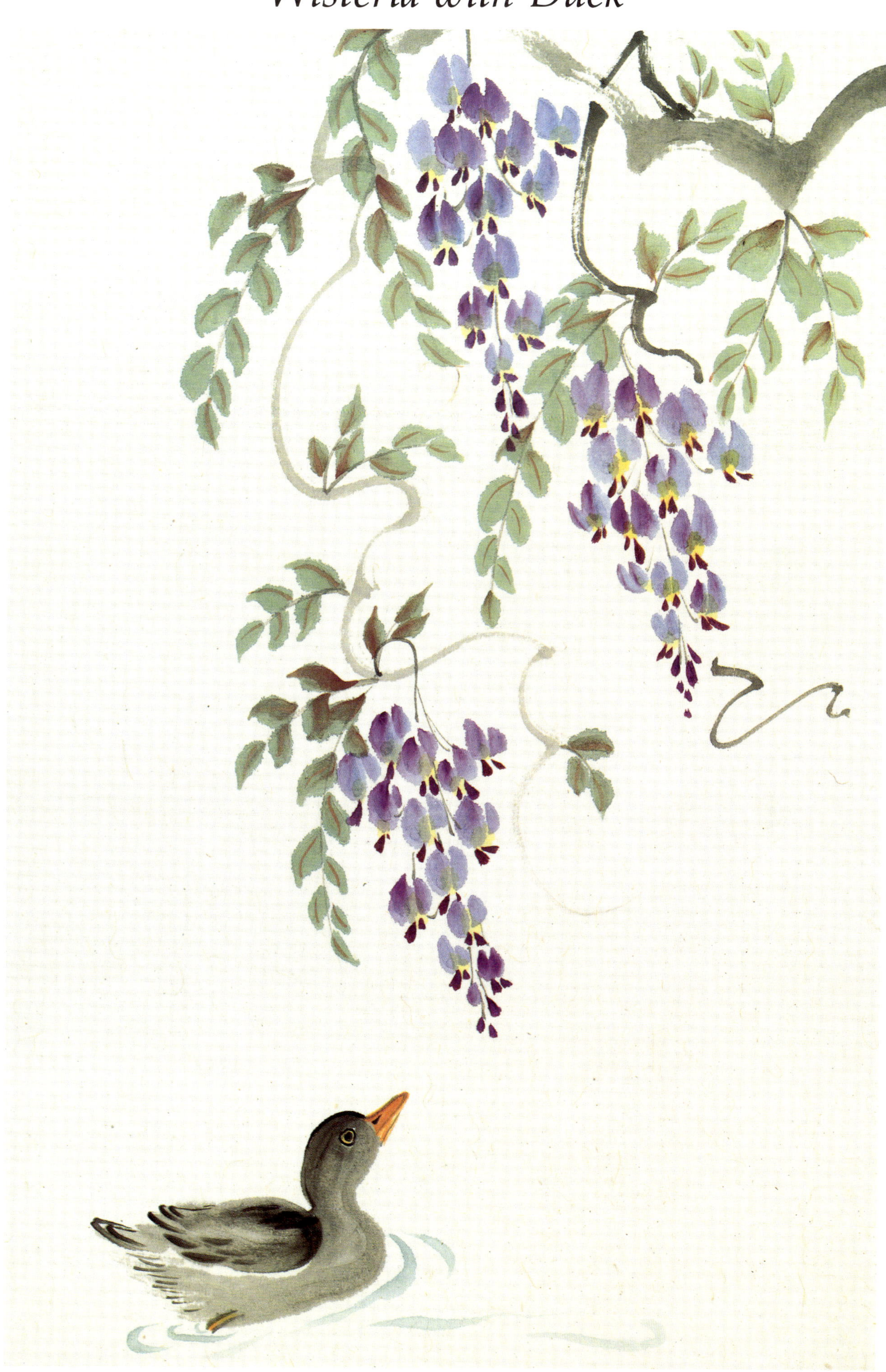

Bauhinia

Bauhinia is one of my favourite Hong Kong flowers. It used to grow wild on the hillside near our house coming into flower in April on small trees. The flowers are pink or white. The leaves are very distinctive as they look like 2 semi-circles joined at one end. The Bauhinia is sometimes referred to as the national flower of Hong Kong.

I painted the flower first with a pale mixture of Peony Purple and Blood Red. The petals are painted towards the centre and the brush pressure is important here, starting light, then increasing and gradually decreasing again. Two strokes are needed for each petal. The central petals have veins added in Peony Purple and Blood Red and the other petals have White veins. Use Teppachi White.

The stamens, consisting of one long one (white) and five shorter ones, are painted in Rattan Yellow and White mixed, with the tip added in Blood Red mixed with a little black ink.

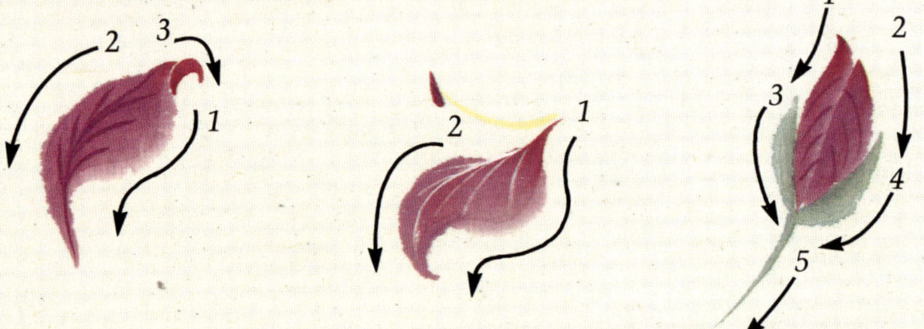

Paint the branch in shades of Autumn Brown with a 'dry' brush and finally paint the leaves using your brush on its side but varying the pressure again. The green is Indigo and Rattan Yellow mixed. Add the veins in Indigo when the leaves are still slightly damp.

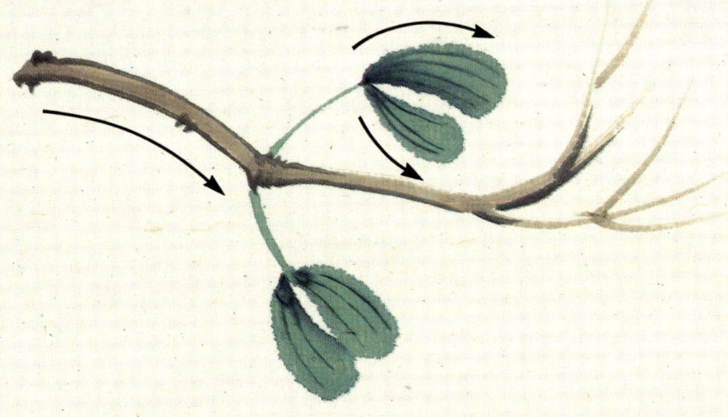

Bauhinia

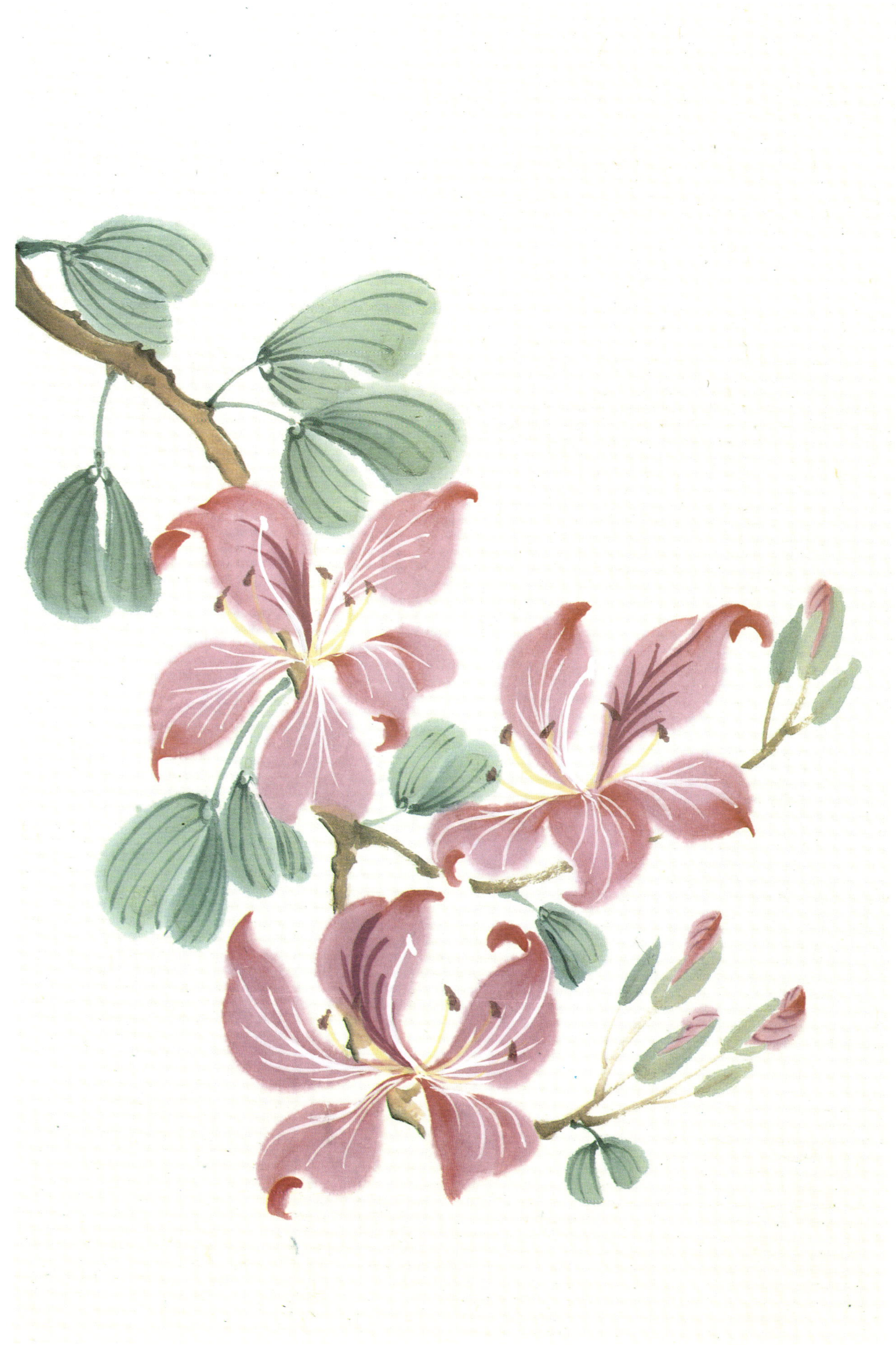

Western Flowers

Although I know this may be frowned upon by some traditionalists I cannot ignore the beauty of the flowers that appear in my garden and the surrounding countryside each year.

This keeps Chinese painting alive for me. By using traditional Chinese methods I have shown my enjoyment of painting on the following four pages. I have deliberately given no instructions so that if you wish to copy them, yours will be different and original.

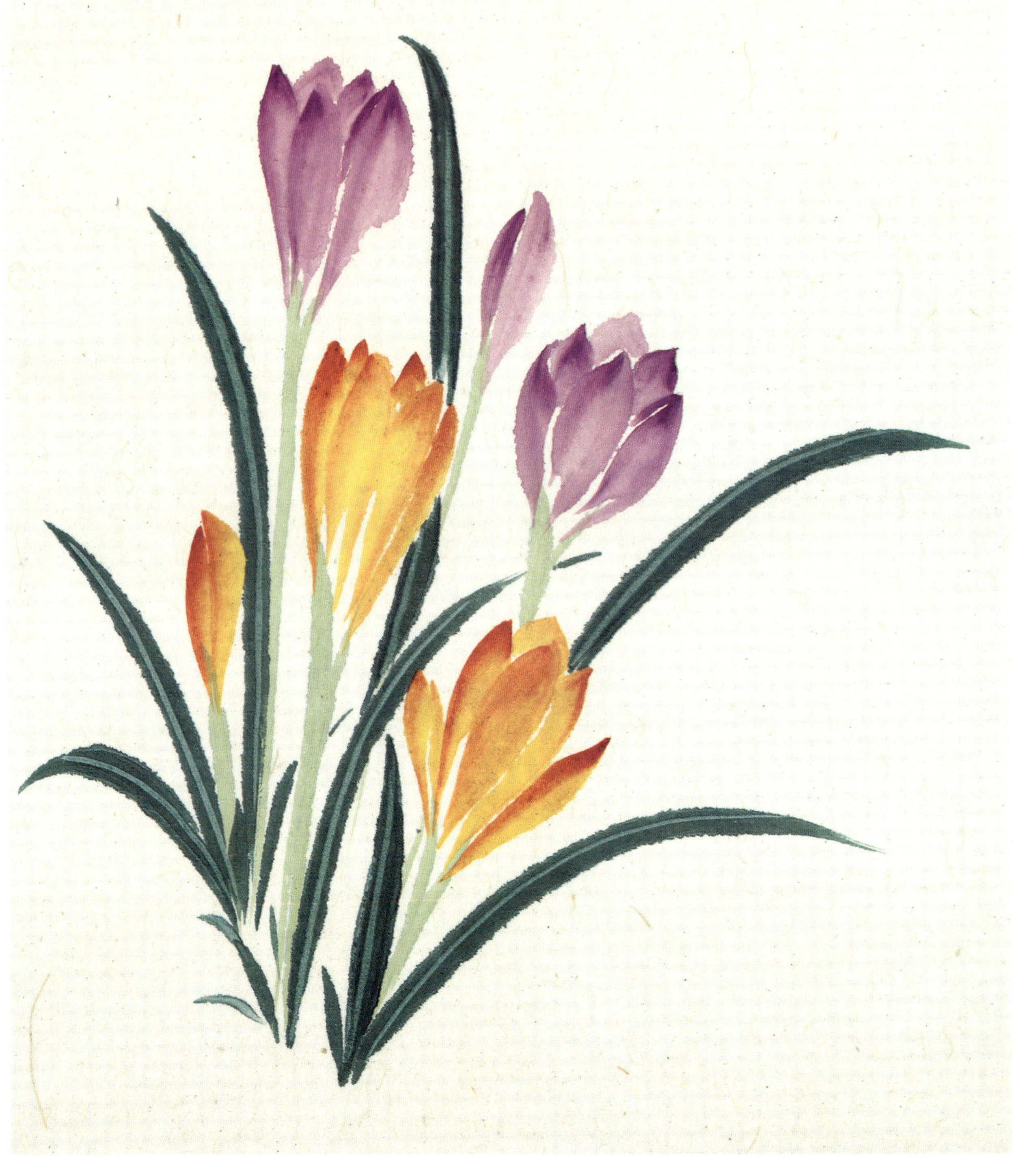

Fuchsia

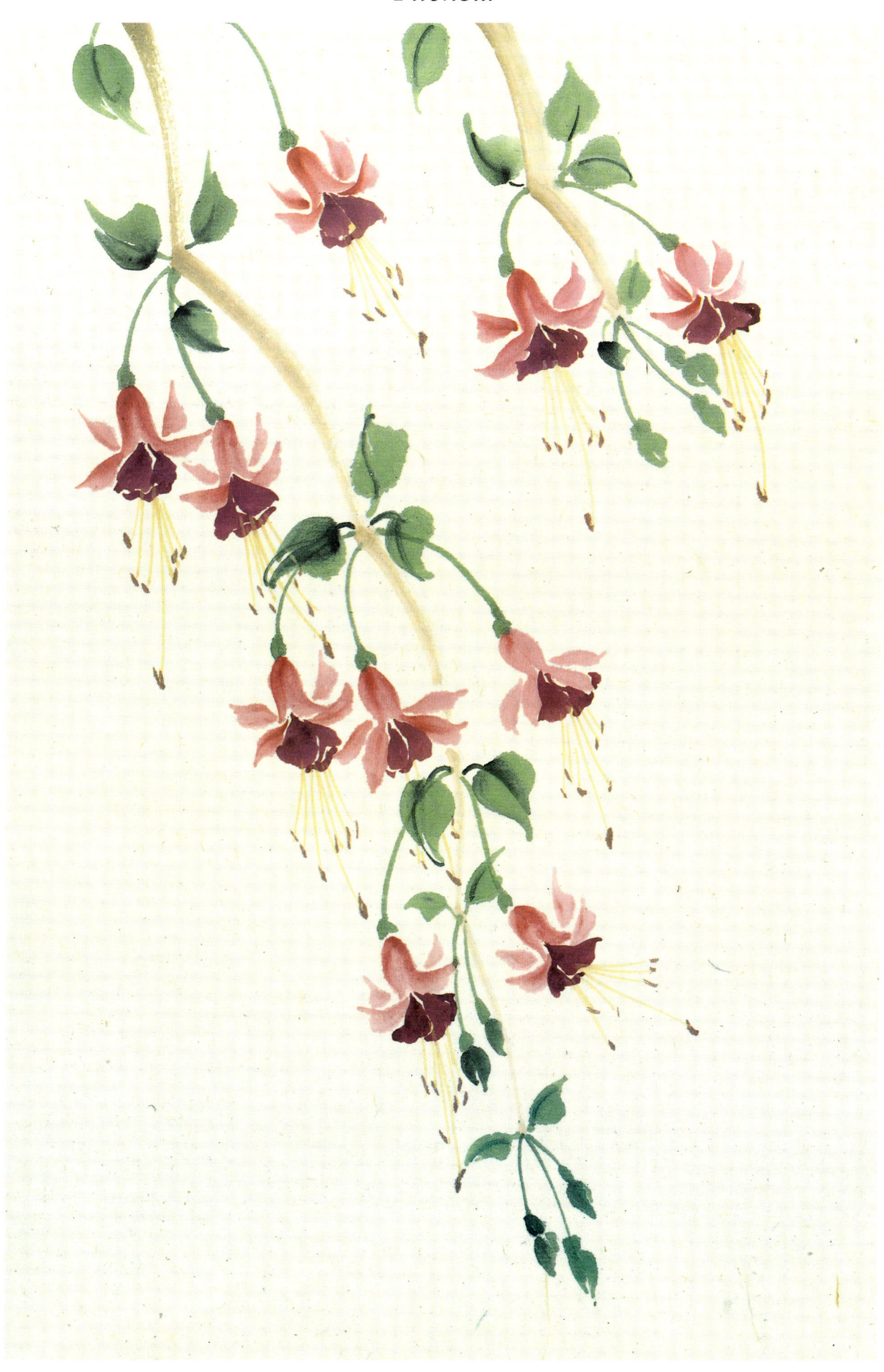

Nasturtium

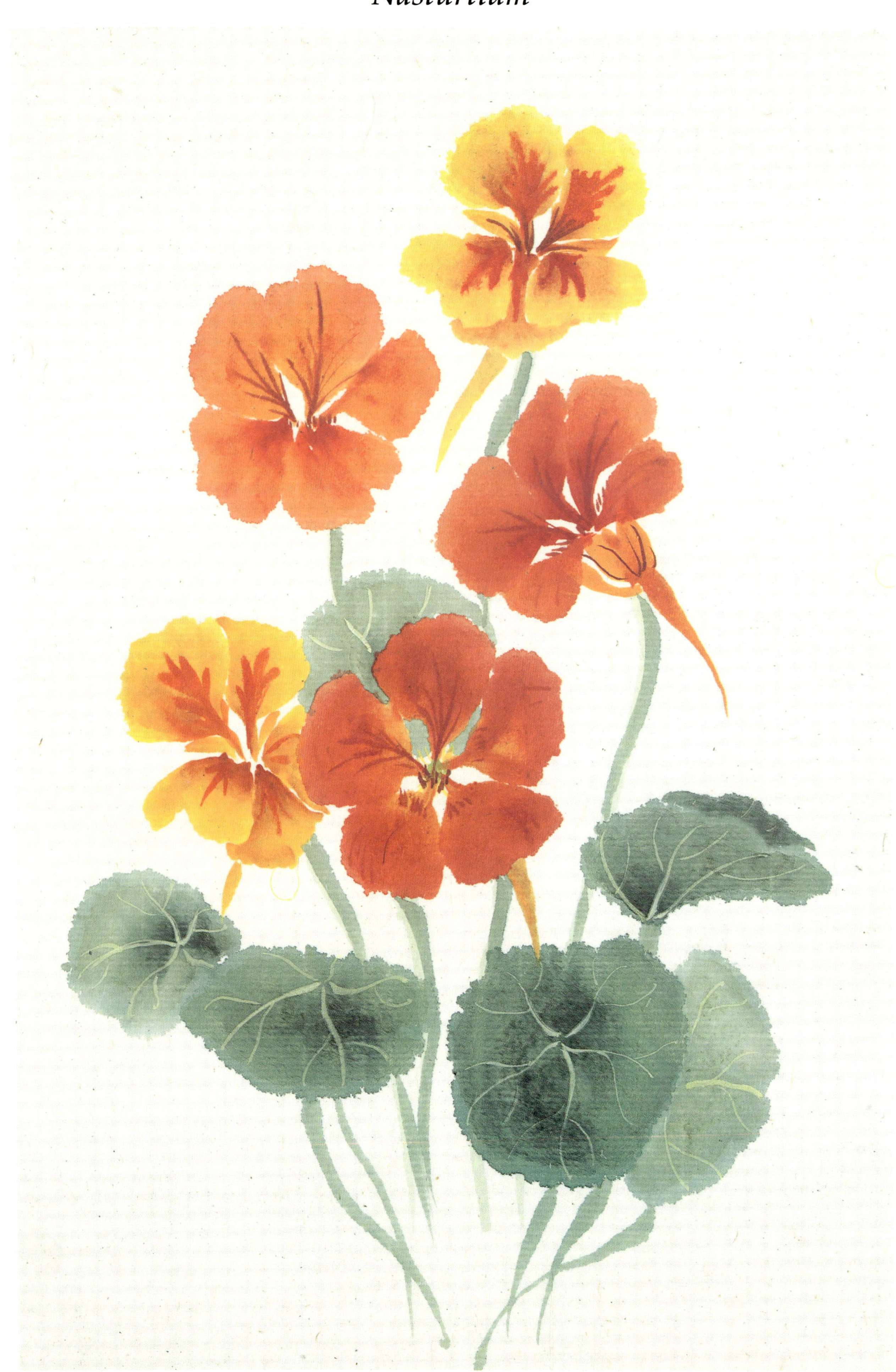

Poppy

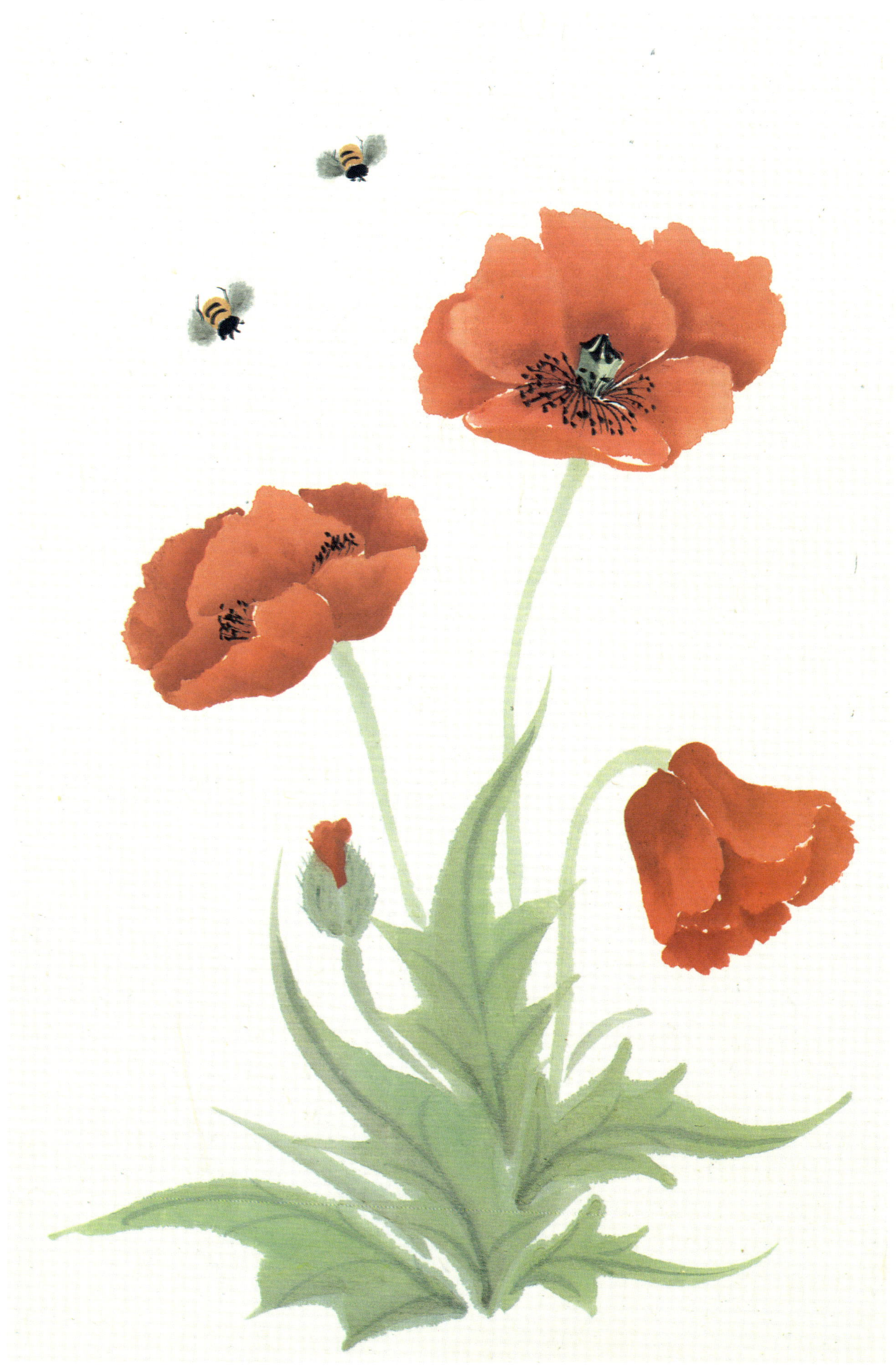

Wash Techniques

I paint washes either with a Hake brush or natural sponge on the front or back of the painting depending on the effect required.

You will find your rice paper infinitely versatile. I do find 'HSUAN' paper is more satisfactory as the 'MOON PALACE' is inclined to scuff with constant wetting. You must be prepared to experiment as I have done, as many of the best results are obtained by mistake! When painting a wash with a brush dampen your paper first to obtain a more even effect.

When using white for snow or moonlight (see page 34) I painted the wash on the back after I have painted the picture as this makes the white really stand out.

For the pine cones I used tea as a backwash. I save my 'dregs' from the teapot and put this in a saucepan with an extra teabag which I then bring to the boil and continue boiling for a minute or two. Remove the teabag (without piercing it) and leave to cool.

When painting washes it is better to use several pale coats of colour remembering to leave each coat to dry first.

Wisteria with Wash

For this painting I sponged the wash onto the front of the paper first using blue, green and mauve in very pale shades. To obtain a stippled effect press very lightly with the sponge.

When the wash was dry I painted the wisteria using the same technique as page 25. To give the painting more depth I painted in some paler flowers and leaves afterwards.

You should be aware that the paper will have a less absorbent texture after the wash has been applied.

Wisteria with Wash

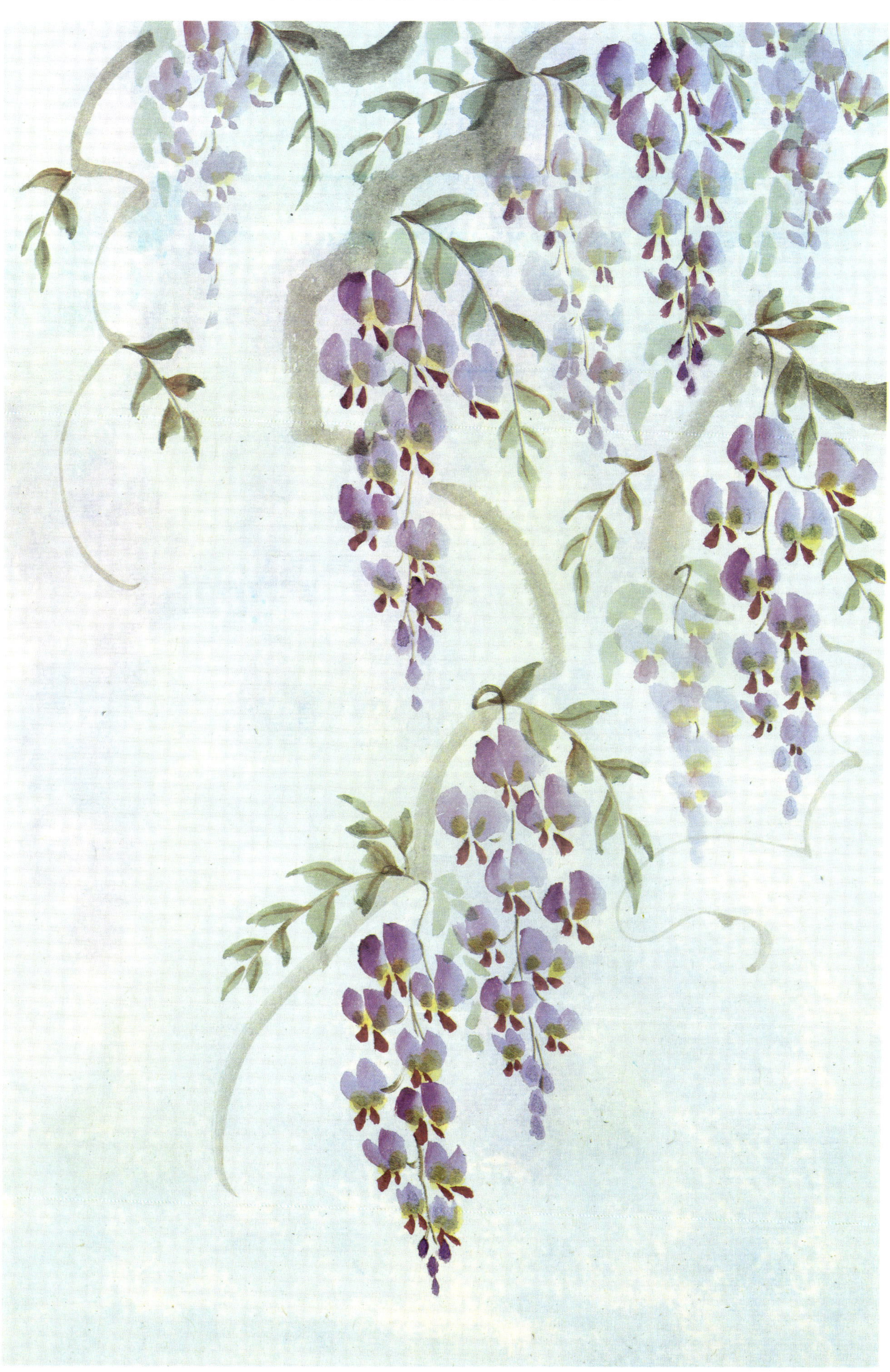

Backwash Ideas

Bamboo in Snow

First paint the bamboo stems and leaves — leave to dry. Flick on white paint with care or you will end up with more on you! When this is dry turn the painting over and brush the wash on the back using a pale shade of Indigo and black ink.

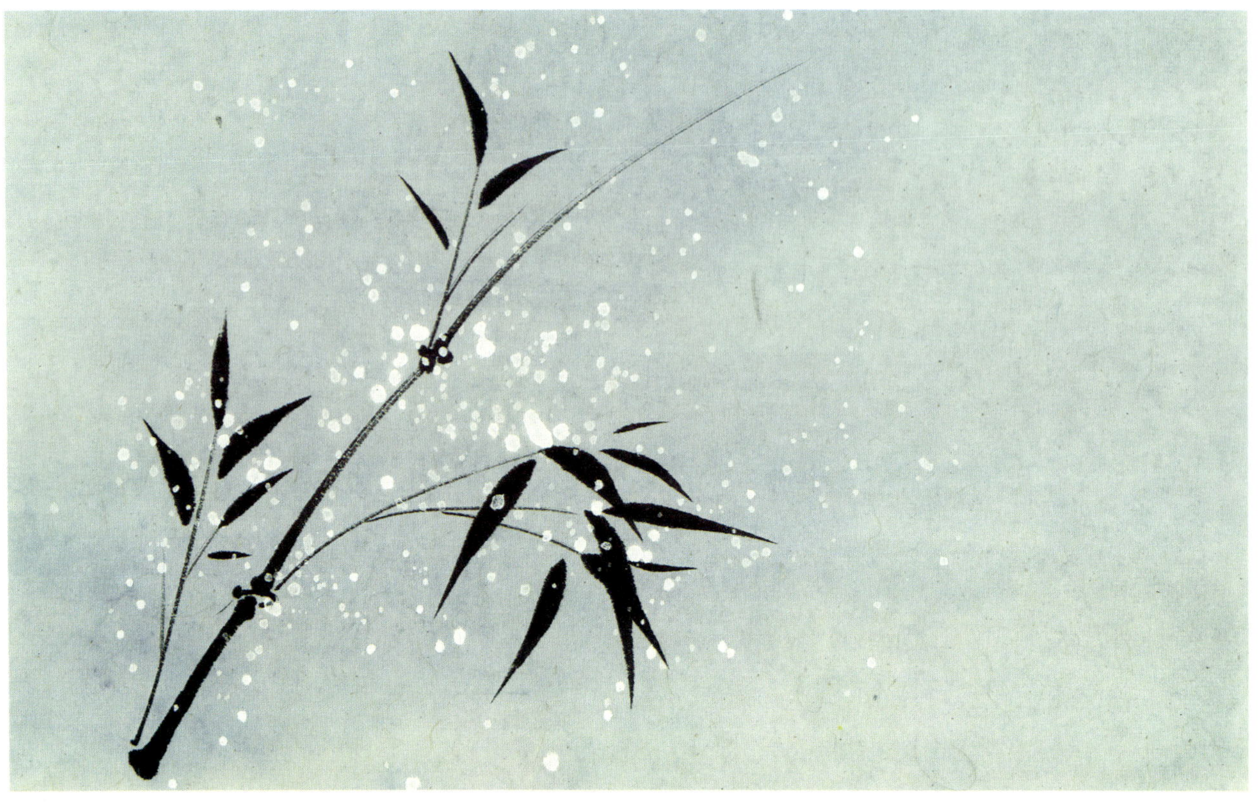

Pine Cones in Snow with tea back wash

Paint the pine cones in black or dark brown. The stroke is rather like a tick with a little more pressure used towards the point of the V. Dab on white paint as above and brush on tea wash (see page 32) when dry.

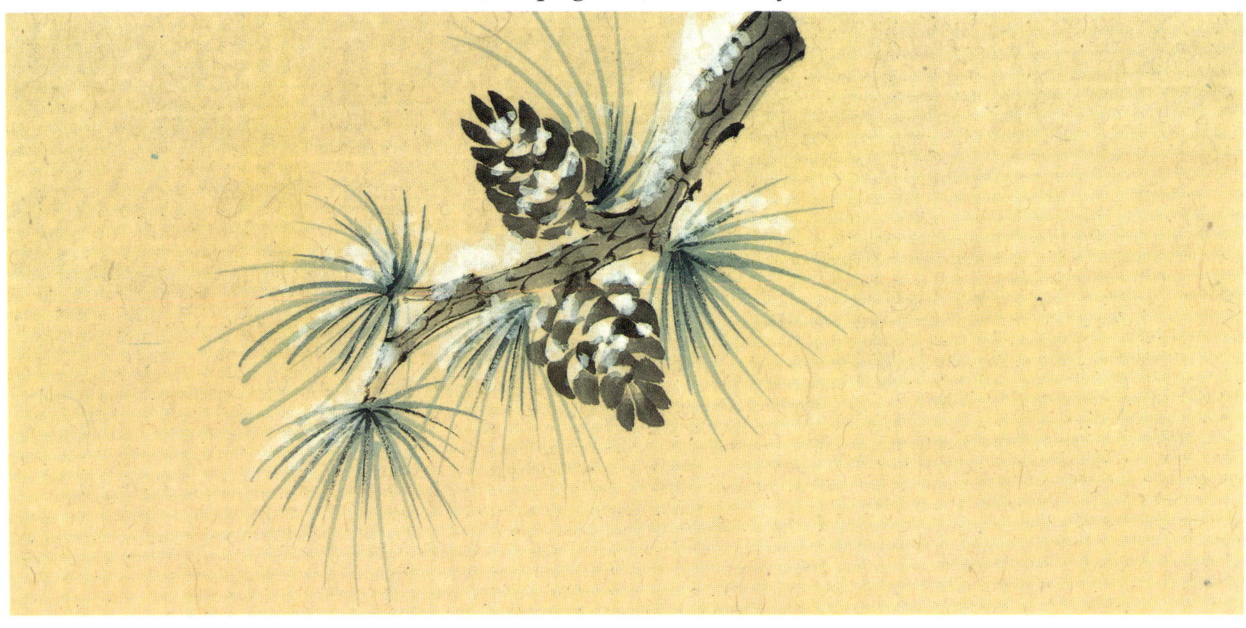

Simple Landscapes

I have included a few very simple landscape ideas on the following pages.

The Chinese took landscape painting much more seriously than other subjects. Landscapes were a symbol of free man. China suffered much strife throughout her history and artists who had been employed as court painters would escape and live a hermit-like existence in the country. As they wandered they would absorb the atmosphere and then return to their studios and paint their impressions. Much of their own feelings would be evident in their work. A disillusioned, angry man might paint his trees leafless and spiky. Landscapes were painted on either vertical or horizontal scrolls — the latter sometimes told a story rather like the Bayeux tapestry.

Those of you who have been lucky enough to visit China will know that the landscape paintings are more true to life than they look.

As a beginner it is as well to paint the landscape in outline first and then add the colour as a wash.

Simple Landscapes

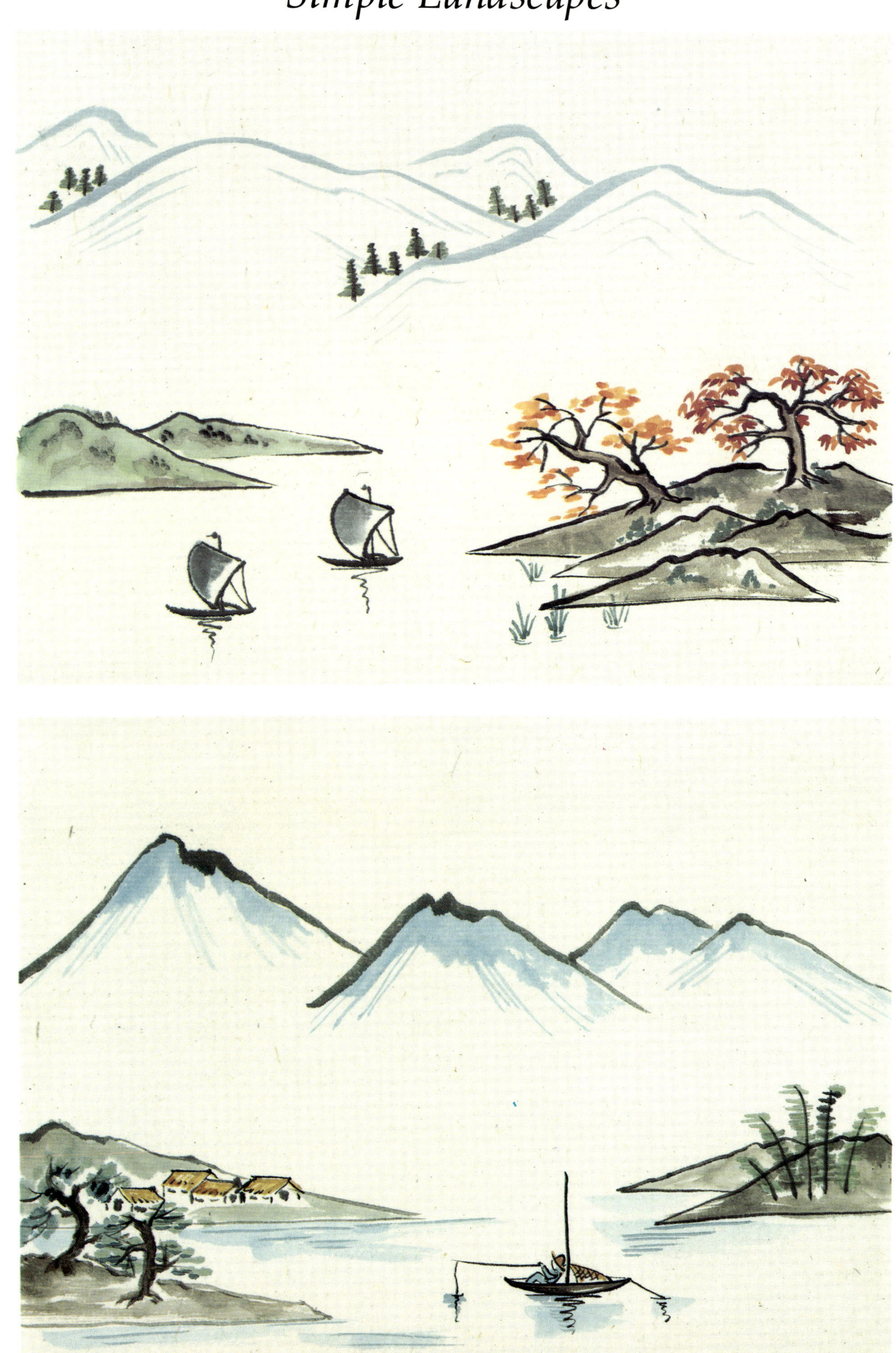

Simple Landscapes

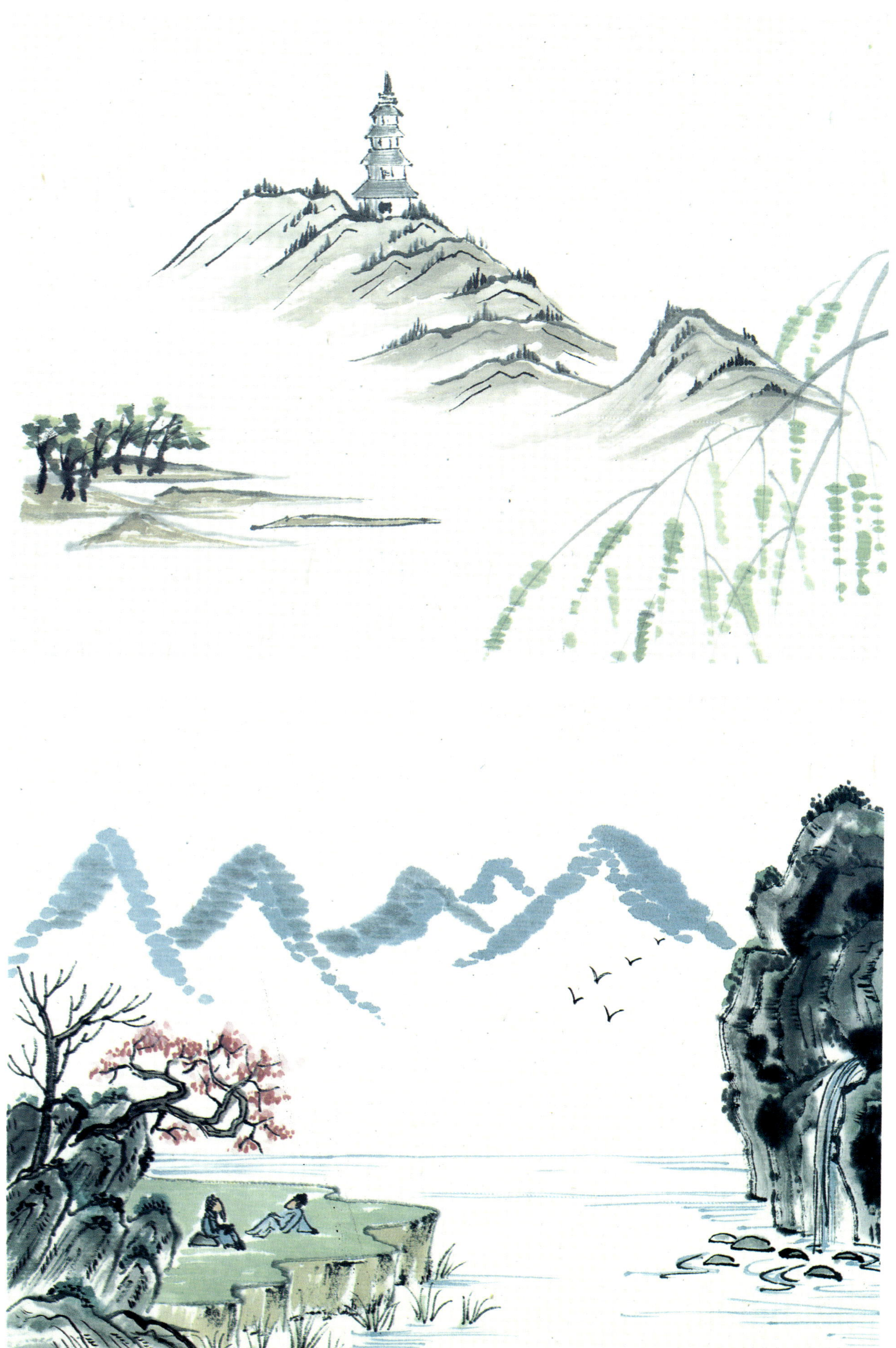

Calligraphy

Because the Chinese calligraphy has always been painted with a brush it is an essential part of painting. The strokes used in calligraphy are extended into the painting. A bamboo painting is supposed to feature all the calligraphy strokes. Practise in this gives you good discipline for your painting.

There are various different styles of calligraphy. At school one learns 'Kai shu', a very disciplined, precise form. 'Running' and 'Grass' styles are much more flee-flowing and often used on paintings when an artist writes his name and explains his painting, often in poetry. Seals are written with the special 'seal script;' a diagrammatic style. (See page 9.)

Although there are thousands of characters they are not all entirely different. There is only a set number of strokes used. The character 'Yung' seen below left uses all the calligraphy strokes. Two simple characters may be written together to give a different meaning (below right).

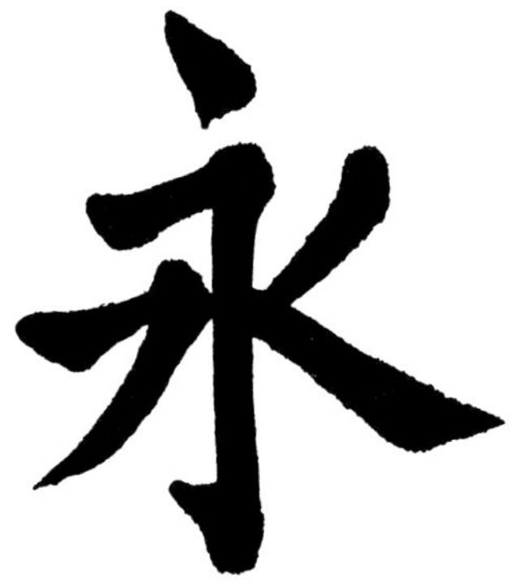

Kai Shu

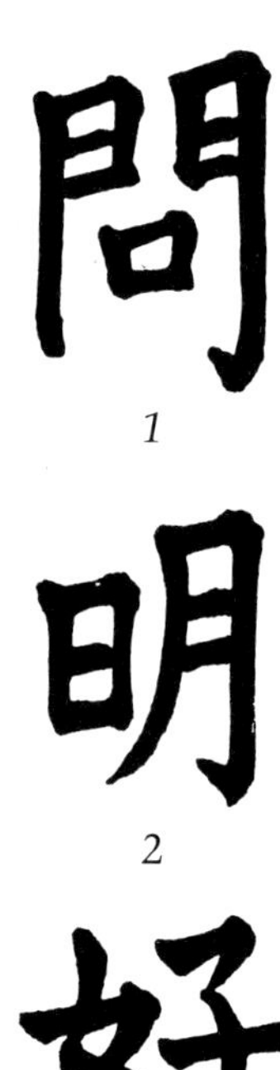

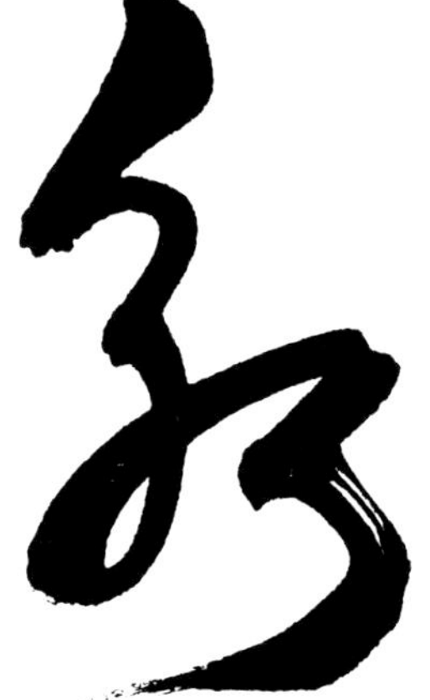

Running

Combination Characters

1) *The character for door with the character for mouth together mean 'ask'.*
2) *'Day' or 'sun' (left) and 'night' or 'moon' (right) together mean bright.*
3) *'Mother' (left) with 'child' (right) form the character 'good'.*

Calligraphy

On this page I have included some phrases for you to write on your pictures. Never write the calligraphy too large — it should not dominate the picture.

蘭竹

1

梅雀爭春

2

松鼠葡萄

3

紫藤

鴨

4

紫荊

5

山明水秀

6

1 *Orchid and bamboo*
2 *Plum blossoms and bird competing for Spring*
3 *Squirrel and grapes*
4 *Wisteria* *Duck*
5 *Bauhinia*
6 *Bright mountains clear water (landscape)*

Calligraphy by Man Yee Moon

Ideas for Cards

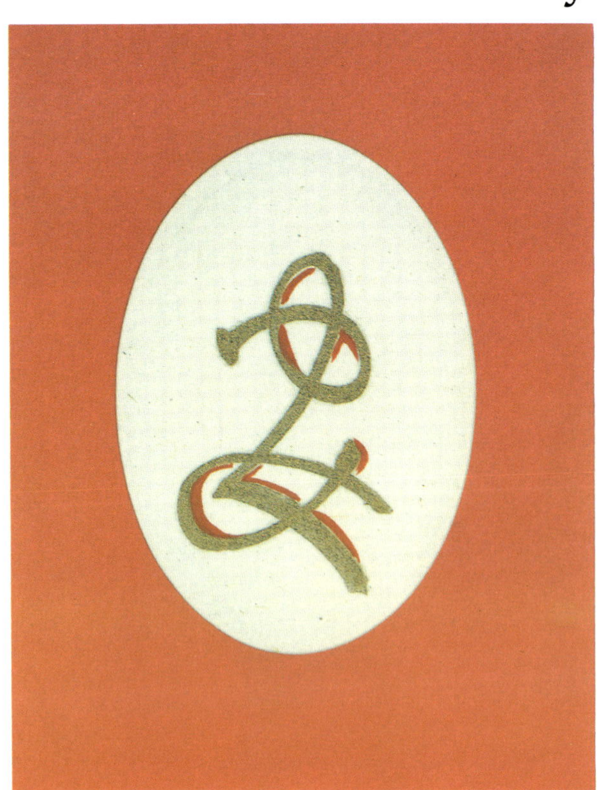

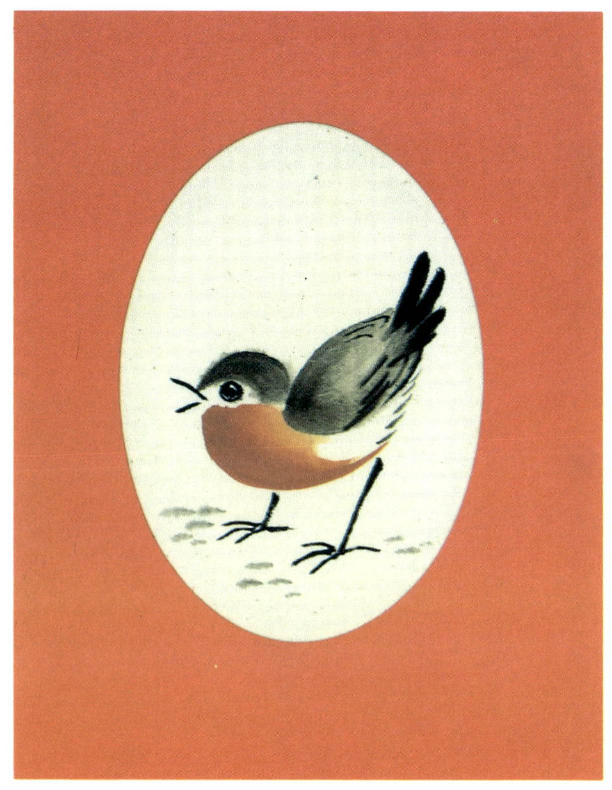

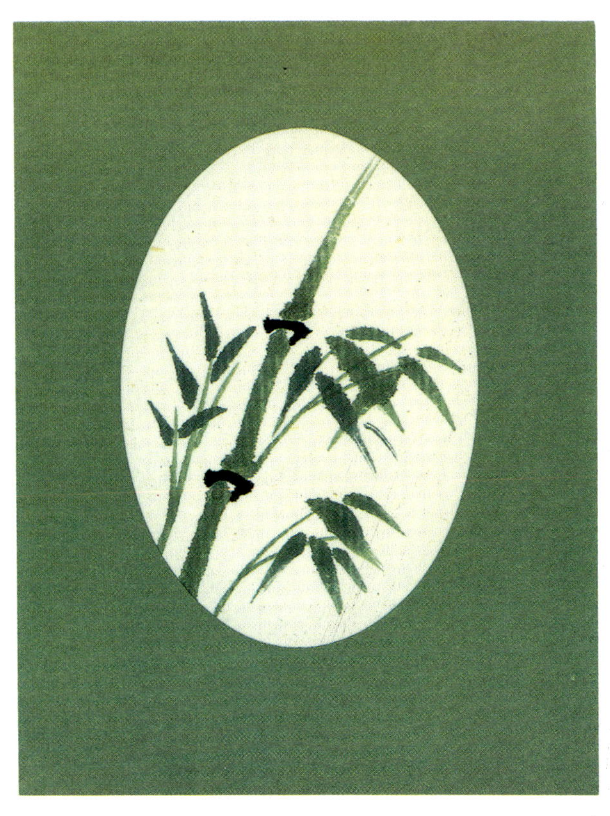

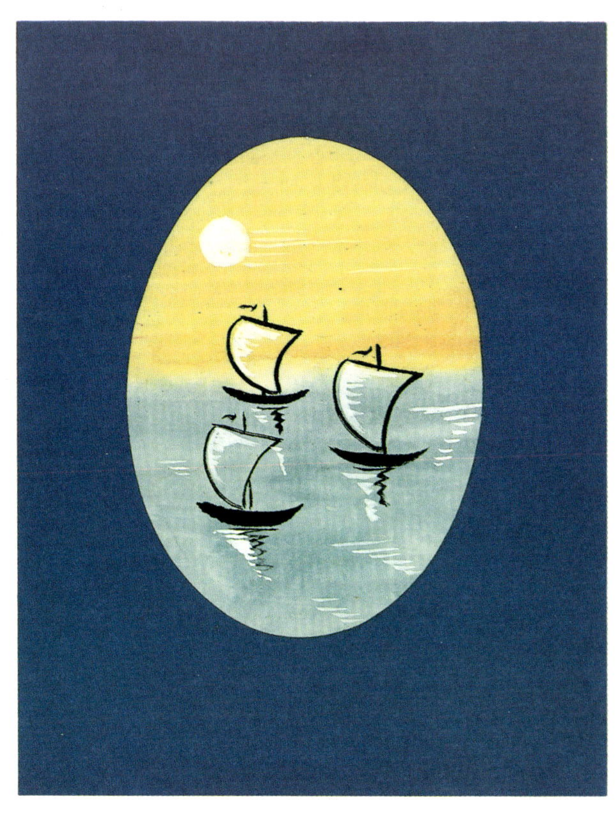